ZARTAR

**TABULA ASIAE**   Ruscelli c. 1565

The early map-makers of Europe were in agreement concerning
the situation of Armenia in the Ancient World. ARMENIA MINOR
lay between the Euphrates River and the Taurus Mountains while
ARMENIA MAJOR, of which only a portion is shown on this map,
stretched eastward from the Euphrates into the Caucasus. These
lands were Armenian for fifteen hundred years before the first
Turkic tribespeople arrived from Central Asia.

# ARMENIAN RUGS
# FROM
# THE GREGORIAN COLLECTION

Arthur T. Gregorian
Joyce Gregorian Hampshire
Photographs by Douglas A. Christian

1987

Endpaper Design by Peg Michel, from embroideries by
Arthur T. Gregorian's mother, Zartar Badalbo'etsi

PRINTED IN NEEDHAM, MASSACHUSETTS
BY CONGRAF

# CONTENTS

# LIST OF MAPS

# AUTHORS' FOREWORD:
## DEFINING THE ARMENIAN RUG

I   Arthur T. Gregorian

In the fifty years I have spent as a dealer and a collector of Oriental Rugs, I have always been aware of the existence of Armenian Rugs hidden under various place names. In the commercial rug trade, rugs are identified by the city or region in which they are made, not by the race or culture of the weaver. Since Armenians in modern times have been scattered throughout the rug-weaving world, most of their rugs have been dealt with under various place names. They have not been recognized or studied as Armenian creations.

Recently an Armenian woman came into my shop in Massachusetts. She was carrying a small rug of obviously Anatolian type. The wool was a little unusual: the rug's story even more so. It seems that this woman's mother and aunt, refugees from the 1915 massacres, had continued to weave rugs after settling in the United States. After long hours in the factory these women would come home and complete nine rows of knots each night. What is the name for such a rug? Anatolian? American? Or Armenian?

Most Armenian rugs are from Turkey, the Caucasus and Persia. The greatest number are from the central and southern Caucasus, the Armenian homeland. In these rugs, as in the rugs from Persia, Armenian weavers show free self-expression, often weaving short messages with dates and signatures. In Armenian rugs from Turkey this never has been the case. There, any rugs too obviously Armenian ran the risk of official confiscation on grounds of containing secret messages. Government suspicion also put the owner of such a rug at risk. For this reason, Armenian inscriptions that do exist in Turkish rugs have often been obliterated, inked out or woven over in an attempt to make the rug more suitable for public exposure. The Turkoman-type rug from Central Asia (Plate 104) a rug offered for sale in Turkey, is an example. The long and elegant inscription was completely blacked out with ink when I purchased it.

The point is sometimes missed that most Armenians in the Near East were not wealthy merchants, but peasants. The places where these rugs were made are mostly rural, where peasants of many different racial backgrounds had separate villages and orchards, but a common way of life. My own village was near Lake Urmia, an area traditionally part of Greater Armenia, but today part of the Persian Azerbaijan. Persia had little meaning for me as a boy — it was a term that referred to the government. People in my village spoke Assyrian or Armenian, and Azeri Turkish was used in town. We were on good terms with our Azeri Muslim neighbors, and different religions helped each other when times were difficult. But even our good friend and neighbor Mehment Ali could not help us when news of the Armenian massacres trickled down to us. He did what he could and provided us with his best oxen for the journey to safety.

Obviously, not all the rugs from Greater Armenia are the product of Armenians. Azeri Turks, Assyrians, Persians, Kurds and other groups all made rugs in similar styles. However, the rugs chosen for inclusion in my collection bear inscriptions in Armenian, clearly indicating their provenance. It is my hope that some day researchers will be able to use these inscribed rugs as a guide to assessing other rugs similar in type and color, but not inscribed. For now, however, it is enough to be able to show these following rugs as undeniable examples of Armenian creativity.

## II    Joyce Gregorian Hampshire

As may be seen from the antique maps illustrating this book, Armenia once enjoyed prominent status in world geography, if not in world power. Events which took place during the last days of the Ottoman Empire did more than obliterate Armenia from the world's maps. An image of Armenians as pathetic victims of exile and massacre took hold of the world's imagination. Unfortunately it almost completely replaced an earlier awareness of Armenians as a small, proud, independent Christian minority in the Islamic Near East; a nationality survived intact from ancient times, noted for more than a thousand years for learning, architecture and the textile arts.

In three recent exhibits of antiquities, from the Soviet Union, Iran and Turkey, the artifacts of many different cultures were claimed by the political power currently pre-eminent in the area. This is nothing new: it has always been the way of empires to use and take credit for the work of their subjects. One purpose behind the collection of rugs in this book is to help reveal the existance of an Armenian artistic culture standing on its own, identifiable, despite the political dominion of other countries.

Historic 'Greater Armenia' can be outlined on a map, but Armenian sovereignty in the area has been the exception, not the rule. Today's Soviet Armenia contains only a tiny piece of the 'homeland', the area surrounding Lake Sevan. Tradition extends Armenia south past the River Araxes to Lake Urmia. Greater Armenia includes Mount Ararat, still the national symbol of Armenians everywhere, and reaches west to the upper Euphrates River. Rarely have Armenians had political control of this area, but here they have lived for more than two thousand years. The landscape is dotted with massive stone churches and monasteries more than one thousand years old. The cities of Erzerum, Kars and Van — all now part of modern Turkey — were famous Armenian cities, filled with churches (cf. page 30).

Most of the rugs which we picture and describe in the following pages were woven in territory that tradition considers Armenian. Many come from eastern Anatolia, in the vicinity of Kars, others from the region we now know as Karabagh, in the southern part of Greater Armenia. The boldest and most primitive are from the Sevan district, an area where we find many of the place names associated with Kazak rugs: Karachop, Lori Pembak, Gendje, all but the last in modern-day Soviet Armenia.

Also included in the following pages are rugs woven in territory now part of modern Iran. The Persian Azerbaijan is another piece of Greater Armenia: the presence of Armenians and Armenian rugs in this region requires no comment. An explanation is in order for the group of rugs from Feridun, however. In the 16th century, for political reasons having to do with war on Turkey, Shah Abbas the Great forcibly relocated a large population of Armenians to central Iran, where his capital city of Isfahan was located. These people settled on the other side of the Zafidrud River, founding a suburb which they called New Julfa in memory of their lost home in the Caucasus. The Armenians prospered in New Julfa. Armenian craftsmen adorned the buildings of Shah Abbas and also built a great cathedral for themselves on their own side of the river. The Armenian presence in central Iran has remained constant since that time, and many small Armenian villages may be found along the road that leads from Hamadan and the Azerbaijan south to Isfahan. The rugs these Armenians weave speak a new artistic language, reflecting the influence of neighboring Bachtiari and Qashqai tribespeople, as well as local wools and dyes.

In 1979 my family exhibited a collection of inscribed Armenian rugs at Dartmouth College and a small catalogue was printed at that time. In 1983 twenty-six 'Armenian Rugs of the Gregorian Collection' were exhibited at the University of Michigan and an illustrated catalogue in color was issued, in a limited edition. Then in 1984 the Kimbell Art Museum of Ft. Worth opened a magnificent show assembled by the Armenian Rugs Society, entitled 'Weavers, Merchants and Kings: The Inscribed Rugs of Armenia'. Sixty-eight rugs, including 12 from the Gregorian Collection, were presented in a color catalogue and in a show which travelled to Virginia, Washington DC, Massachusetts and California. Despite the interest these shows have aroused, there is nevertheless a small group of art historians who cannot bear to admit the existence of Armenian woven rugs. They go to great lengths to explain away the inscriptions, just as some publishers have gone to great lengths physically to expunge the name 'Armenia' from the map of Asia Minor.

Armenians have been in diaspora for most of their history. They have had to accomodate themselves to the customs and laws of many different lands. Nevertheless they have preserved a sense of their own identity, religion, language, literature and visual arts. Of the 104 rugs published below, 102 bear dates, inscriptions or at the very least initials in Armenian. There is no reason at all not to call them Armenian, unless indeed it is the purpose of some art historians to deny Armenians their culture just as once they were denied, by political policy, their country, homes and lives.

## THE ARMENIAN ALPHABET

| | | | | | |
|---|---|---|---|---|---|
| Ա | ա | aip | Մ | մ | men |
| Բ | բ | pen | Յ | յ | he |
| Գ | գ | kim | Ն | ն | noo |
| Դ | դ | tah | Շ | շ | shah |
| Ե | ե | yech | Ո | ո | vo |
| Զ | զ | zah | Չ | չ | chah |
| Է | է | ai | Պ | պ | bay |
| Ը | ը | yet | Ջ | ջ | chay |
| Թ | թ | to | Ռ | ռ | rrah |
| Ժ | ժ | zhay | Ս | ս | say |
| Ի | ի | ini | Վ | վ | vev |
| Լ | լ | lune | Տ | տ | dune |
| Խ | խ | kh | Ր | ր | ray |
| Ծ | ծ | dzah | Ց | ց | tso |
| Կ | կ | ghen | Ւ | ւ | hune |
| Հ | հ | ho | Փ | փ | pure |
| Ձ | ձ | tsah | Ք | ք | kay |
| Ղ | ղ | ghad | Օ | o | o |
| Ճ | ճ | jay | Ֆ | ֆ | fay |

# A NOTE ON ARMENIAN HISTORY

The Armenians are an ancient race whose roots have begun only recently to be documented by archaeology. Their homeland centered on the fertile valley of Mt. Ararat and extended at one time from the Caucasus to the Mediterranean. They arose from obscurity to become one of the great empires of the ancient world, but their power was short-lived and is largely forgotten by history.

The name "Armenia" is a foreign term, not used by the Armenians themselves. It was first recorded in 521 BC at Behistun, where the great Persian King Darius had cut into rock a record of his victories. One of the countries under his domination was Armenia. Armenians refer to themselves as "Hai" and to their country as "Hayistan."

Ancient Armenia reached its zenith under the most famous of its kings, Tigranes the Great (95-55 BC). His conquests extended from the Caucasus to the Pontic Alps and from the Mediterranean to the Euphrates. He brought craftsmen from every corner of his vast empire to embellish his capital city of Tigrakerta (Diyarbekir) in the Euphrates Valley. Greek mercenaries opened his gates to the attacking Romans in 69 BC however, and Tigranes' empire became a part of the Roman one, paying an annual levy of 5000 talents.

The turning point in Armenian history came more than three centuries later. In 301 AD King Tiridates was converted to Christianity by St. Gregory the Illuminator, and Armenia became the first nation in the world to become Christian. In 404 AD, the Armenian monk Mesrop Mashtots invented a phonetic alphabet for Armenian; he also created alphabets for the neighboring Georgians and Albanians. By 436 AD the Bible had been translated into Armenian, and churches and monasteries were being built. This was the start of a great flowering of Armenian learning and scholarship, and of decorative arts, notably architecture, sculpture and illumination of manuscripts.

In 451 AD the Persians, who were at this time Zoroastrian, decided to subjugate Armenia and sever its political and religious ties with Byzantium and the West. 65,000 Armenians under the leadership of Prince Vartan Mamagunian resisted an invading force of more than 200,000. Persia ultimately bowed to this obstinacy, accepting an annual tribute and not pushing the religious matter any further. This, the first battle ever fought to preserve Christianity, is looked upon by Armenians everywhere as a sacred event.

Both the Byzantine Greeks and the Arab armies of Islam overran Armenia during the next few centuries. In 813 AD the Bulgarian armies carried off among their spoils from Armenia a large inventory of carpets. In the same period the Arab geographer al-Ishtakhri wrote of "Dabil" (Dvin)

> . . . in this town are made woolen garments and rugs,
> cushions, seats, laces and other items of Armenian
> manufacture. From them is also obtained the dye
> named "kirmiz" and cloth is dyed with it . . . Dabil is
> the capital of Armenia and there stays Sanbat
> (Sembat I) . . .

Kirmiz is a crimson similar to the cochineal of the New World, a famous
and favored color of ancient Armenia. Later in the 9th century another
Arab geographer Ibn-Hauqal elaborated:

> . . . as for the items called "Armenian weaving," they
> are . . . rugs, covers and cushions. There is none
> equal to them among the things of this world from
> end to end.

One inventory list of tribute paid by Armenians at this time includes
twenty large carpets along with fish, mules and falcons.

Finally, in the 11th century, the Seljuk Turks from Central Asia destroyed Armenia's greatest city of Ani. The Seljuks settled in eastern
Anatolia, confronting the Byzantines, while Armenian refugees fled
the area, some going as far as Poland and Egypt.

When the Crusaders arrived in Cilicia — a strategic area surrounding the
Gulf of Alexandretta, including the cities of Adana and Tarsus — they
were pleased to find themselves welcomed by a substantial Christian
population of Armenians. Small dynasties of Armenian land-owners and
princely houses were gaining wider and wider control in Cilicia, until a
true kingdom was established under Levon the Great (1186 -1219) and his
successor Hetum I (1226-1269). The Armenian kingdom of Cilicia was in
correspondence with Rome and the Holy Roman Emperor, and these
European contacts had one small but amusing long-lasting effect: the
assumption by Armenians of the word *baron* as a masculine term of
address.

The next conquerors to come from Central Asia after the Seljuks were
the Mongols. Together with the Mamelukes of Egypt they brought
devastation upon the Crusaders and subjugation to Armenia. During
this period of Mongol supremacy one of the most colorful figures of
Armenian history arose, Constable Sempad, King Hetum's oldest
brother and commander-in-chief of the army. Sempad negotiated an
alliance with the Mongols on a trip to the Mongolian capital in 1246-
1248. He paved the way for his brother the king, who made the trip in
1253-1256 to conclude the treaty. Marco Polo's famous journey fifteen
years later was largely made possible by the existance of this Armeno-
Mongol understanding, which extended from Asia Minor to the far-
flung Empire of the Archers.

Of the Armenian cities he passed while crossing Cilicia, Marco Polo wrote:

> . . . the best and handsomest carpets in the world are
> brought here, and the silks of crimson and other rich

> colors . . . (The local Turks) are rude and dull of
> intellect. They dwell amongst the mountains and in
> places difficult of access where their object is to find
> good pasture for their animals.

The help which Armenians had offered the Crusaders was to pay off in trade agreements. By 1345 Armenians had received permission to sell carpets on the steps of the Cathedral in Bruges. Trade with the Lowlands flourished for centuries. Armenian merchants imported Turkish, Armenian, Caucasian and Persian products on a regular basis, with additional trade centers in Italy, France and Spain. By 1660 there were more than 60 Armenian establishments in Amsterdam. The rugs they sold to Europe have been preserved for us in the meticulous and detailed paintings of the Dutch masters.

Meanwhile, in Asia Minor, the Osmanli or Ottoman Turks had followed in the steps of the Seljuks and the Mongols. By the 16th century the Ottoman Sultan Selim I had taken possession of most of the Armenian lands in eastern Anatolia, as far as present-day Kurdistan. This formed an important buffer against the Persians. In 1639, border disputes finally culminated in an agreement which divided Armenia into two parts. Anatolian Armenia fell to the Ottomans while Caucasian Armenia went to Persia. To this day lingusitic and cultural differences persist between Western and Eastern Armenians.

The 16th and 17th centuries saw further dispersion of Armenians in the Middle East. Shah Abbas relocated a large population of Armenians from Julfa to Isfahan and a century later, in 1747, Nadir Shah moved another large group from the same area to the Holy City of Meshed, on the eastern borders of Iran. In both places they settled and practiced their religion and their trades.

When the Romanoff Tsars extended their power into the Transcaucasus during the early 19th century, Armenians looked for a close relationship with their new Christian overlords. Through Russia, Armenians once again came into close contact with the west, at a time when many revolutionary theories of government were being formed. Armenian intellectuals, like others throughout Europe, formed idealistic societies which embraced the principles of socialism and anarchy. To the fiercely insular and conservative Ottoman Turks, the new and dangerous ideas of Russian Armenians made all Armenians suspect. It is to this period that so many Armenian rugs of Franco-Russian influence belong, many of which are dominated by the rose motif, the rose being an ancient symbol for Armenia.

At the end of the Russo-Turkish War in 1878 the Armenians within the Ottoman Empire became scapegoats for its defeat. As official persecution increased, Ottoman Armenians appealed to Europe for intercession and this was considered the final proof of treachery. Civil turmoil in 1895 culminated in a massacre of Armenians that took some 300,000 lives.

Another 30,000 were massacred in Cilicia in 1905. Then during the Great War, in 1915, a mass deportation of Armenians was ordered with hundreds of thousands of uprooted Armenians being marched into the desert to die. Nearly two million Armenians lost their lives, through murder, starvation, torture and mass deportation. Intellectuals and civic leaders were the first to suffer, but the killing spread to include simple villagers and illiterate peasants. Entire towns were destroyed. Those who survived fled to other parts of the Middle East, to southeast Asia, to Europe and the Americas.

Thousands came to the United States, and today there are about half a million Americans of Armenian descent. But the greatest concentration of Armenians world-wide is in the Soviet Socialist Republic of Armenia, a land to which many Armenians returned from diaspora. But, wherever Armenians have settled, they have continued to be artists, artisans and merchants, following their traditional occupations. Armenian surnames reflect the trades of past Armenians: Najarian (carpenter), Kazanjian (kettle-maker), Zildjian (cymbal-maker), Nalbandian (blacksmith), Tufangian (gunsmith), Nakashian (artist), Boyajian (dyer). Armenian history is as rich in creativity as in trouble: both aspects can be seen in the rugs of this collection.

# THE DATING OF INSCRIBED ARMENIAN RUGS

In many cases the dates shown on Armenian Rugs are followed by the Armenian letter Թ (TIV) or by the word ԱՄԻ or ամի (AMI). AMI is often represented by the monogram Ա̄.

A date followed by TIV may be translated as "on the date —" while a date followed by AMI may be translated as "in that year —." In the following pages TIV and AMI have simply been transliterated.

Another common form is the letter Ի (I) or the letters ԻՆ (IN). This is an ordinal form, e.g. transforming '20' into '20th.' Most dates are written clearly, even where the accompanying inscription is garbled. In a few cases the first or last numeral has been doubled or omitted (v. PLATE 37 and PLATE 65). Memorial rugs stress an exact date, e.g. PLATE 53, and this form is typically Armenian, and may still be seen on Armenian grave-stones. Occasionally the month's name is written out, in part or in full, as in PLATE 57.

The ornate letter forms used in many of the rug inscriptions rivals that of the memorial stone-cutter (see below). A simple, printed form of the Armenian alphabet is reproduced on page 4. Note that on the gravestone shown below shears and a comb are depicted, the symbols of the dead woman's profession. She was a weaver.

Photographed by
Arthur T. Gregorian
in the graveyard of
Rahvar, Urmia, Iran.

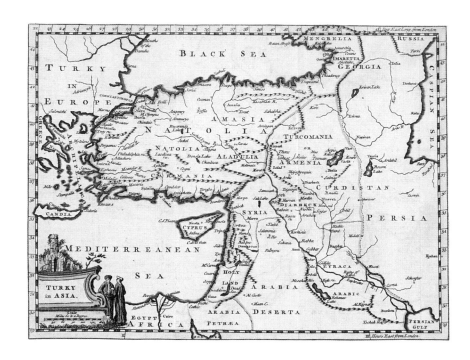

**TURKY IN ASIA**   English Map c. 1770

The traditional west Armenian homeland is shown on this map as
TURCOMANIA OR ARMENIA, reflecting the great influx of Turkic
tribes from Central Asia, which started with the Seljuks in the 11th
century AD. Of this area, KARS in the north, DIARBECK (Diyarbekir)
in the south and VAN in the east are all represented by rugs in the
following pages.

# I: ARMENIAN RUGS OF ANATOLIA

The nine rugs in this section were all woven in territory now a part of modern Turkey. The earliest (Plate 1) is a silk prayer rug, woven in Bursa c.1800. Bursa, on the Sea of Marmora, was a Byzantine city of importance and it retained a sizeable Christian population, both Greek and Armenian, under Ottoman rule. Its reputation as a center for fine textiles was widespread: the most unusual thing about the silk rug in this collection is that its Armenian weaver inscribed it. The eight other rugs are inscribed with dates from 1900-1938, and were woven in a region that embraces the ancient capital of Tigranes the Great, the historic Armenian kingdom of Cilicia and the westernmost part of Greater Armenia. The key cities here are Diyarbekir, Kars and Van: the chief tribal influence Kurdish (Yuruk). The rugs of this region are firm and heavy, simple and geometric. In West Armenian rugs the Turkish preference for tones of gold, green, purple and aubergine seem to have displaced the classic Armenian reds and blues. The fine silk jejim from Van (Plate 9) is a notable exception.

Armenians who fled Anatolia during the First World War could bring little with them; treasured among such families are examples of Armenian flat-work, both kilim and jejim, light enough in texture and small enough in size to be easily carried. Most rugs were left behind, some buried for safe-keeping as will be noted below. Since these Armenian flat-woven textiles are not inscribed, they lie outside the scope of this book, despite their unquestioned provenance. Pictured below is one such item, a classic Peasant apron from the vicinity of Van. It is similar to the garment shown in the engraving of 1862, reproduced on p. 164.

## PLATE 1: **BURSA** "PRAYER RUG" (SILK)

4'1" x 6'2"

Ca. 1800, Inscribed
INSCRIPTION: **HENA ZAND**

During the 18th and 19th centuries, finely woven rugs were made in Istanbul, Hereke and in Bursa, the old Ottoman capital. The Armenian weaver of this fine silk rug has signed her name, "The Obedient One" in the main field under the columns. It is possible that the rug was originally woven for use in an Armenian church rather than as a Muslim prayer rug. In the Ottoman Empire, the development of the design of the Islamic prayer rug has obvious roots in Greek and Armenian ecclesiastical art. The arches, pillars, cypress trees, urns and hanging lanterns familiar to us in so may beautiful Islamic prayer rugs can be found in early Byzantine and Armenian illuminated manuscripts as well as in decorative stone carving. In this example cypress trees signifying eternity frame a central niche, in which the life force is characterized by a vase of flowers.

It should be borne in mind that old silk rugs are notorious for their fragility and the fugitive nature of many of their dyes. This lovely rug now carries with it only a ghost of its original, much more vivid beauty.

PLATE 1

BURSA "PRAYER RUG" (SILK)   4'1" x 6'2"
Ca. 1800, Inscribed

COLORS:   Pale gold, yellow gold, rust, medium and light blue, red.

WARP:       SILK, TAN, 2 STRANDS, Z-SPIN, S-PLY

WEFT:       SILK, IVORY, 2 STRANDS, Z-SPIN, S-PLY, 2 SHOOTS

PILE:        SILK

KNOT:       GHIORDES, ca. 414/inch

EDGES:      FLAT, GOLD

ENDS:       NOT ORIGINAL

PREVIOUSLY PUBLISHED: The Gregorian Collection of Armenian Rugs (Dartmouth);
Weavers, Merchants and Kings (Fort Worth).

## PLATE 2: **KARS** "LESHGI STAR DESIGN"

4′ x 15′9″

Dated 1900
INSCRIPTION: **I. 1900 AMI**

The "Leshgi" star has traditionally been associated with the Kuba district. However, it is an old design and widely popular. Many inscribed Armenian examples are known; one from the Caucasus and two from the Azerbaijan are included in this book (cf. Plates 30, 91, 92). The motif is an ornate variation on a classic theme, that is a diagonal cross superimposed on an equilateral cross, the whole figure enclosed within a stepped medallion. The so-called "sunburst design" ( cf. Plates 3 and 90) is a related form.

This rug, quite plain in both design and color, is from the region of Kars. At one time it was badly damaged and later patched: it is likely that this is another of the rugs buried for safe-keeping during the war and massacres. Rugs from this region are noted for their heavy feel and hard, resilient wool; despite its damage this rug is still strong and serviceable.

PLATE 2

KARS "LESHGI STAR DESIGN"    4' x 15'9"
Dated 1900

COLORS (faded):    Henna, rose, dark and light blue, gold, dark brown, tan.

WARP:    WOOL, BROWN AND TAN, 3 STRANDS, Z-SPIN, S-PLY

WEFT:    WOOL, BROWN AND RED, 2 STRANDS, Z-SPIN, S-PLY, 2 SHOOTS

PILE:    WOOL, 2 STRANDS, Z-SPIN, S-PLY

KNOT:    GHIORDES, ca. 49/inch

EDGES:    FLAT, ROSE

ENDS:    KILIM; UNRAVELLED

## PLATE 3: **KARS** "MODIFIED SUNBURST DESIGN"

4' x 9'3"

Dated 1902 and Inscribed
INSCRIPTION: **1902 AMI MAKOR**

In addition to the usual goats and birds, the weaver (Makor, "clean") of this rug has included two uniformed soldiers, arms akimbo, with tall black boots and shiny buttons. The three medallions are shaped like orthodox crosses, similar to the design called "sunburst" (cf. Plate 90) but lacking the radiating arms at the corner. These radiating arms are themselves remnants of an overlying diagonal cross, and their presence in this design is recalled by the four pairs of motifs which resemble pointing arrows in boxes. Diamonds within the main medallions enclose a flowering branch, the arms of which terminate in small equilateral crosses. The colors of this rug are typical of the area near Sivas, but the heavy weave and geometric pattern are classically Kars.

PLATE 3

KARS "MODIFIED SUNBURST DESIGN"   4' x 9'3"
Dated 1902 and Inscribed

COLORS:   Red, gold, aniline purple, tan, dark brown, pink, ivory.

WARP:      WOOL, RED AND WHITE,*

WEFT:      WOOL*

PILE:       WOOL*

KNOT:      GHIORDES*

EDGES:     FLAT, DARK BROWN AND PINK

ENDS:      KILIM FOLDED AND SEWN

PREVIOUSLY PUBLISHED: The Gregorian Collection Of Armenian Rugs (Dartmouth)

* Rug unavailable for technical analysis

## PLATE 4: **KARS**

3'2" x 11'6"

Dated 1904 and Inscribed
INSCRIPTION: **1904 AMI**
**THIS RUG BELONGS TO NARINGUL**

This is a simple village rug from the Kars district. The long shape and distinctive pattern of repeated crosses suggests that it might have been intended for use in a church. The letters are large and clear, yet there is the curious fact that the Armenian name "Naringul" is spelt without vowels, in the Arabic fashion, e.g. NRNGL. There is one patch in the field, by the border.

Many Armenian rugs were used in memorial fashion, either woven for that purpose or opportunistically inscribed while on the loom to commemorate a birth, death or wedding. This piece seems to fall into the former category, with the inscription forming the actual design of the rug. Since crosses usually indicate a death, it can be inferred that this rug was woven for a church in memory of a deceased woman named Naringul.

PLATE 4

KARS   3'2" x 11'6"
Dated 1904 and Inscribed

COLORS:   Rose red, gold, dark and light brown, ivory, dusty rose, aniline purple.

WARP:      WOOL, TAN, 3 STRANDS, Z-SPIN, S-PLY

WEFT:       WOOL, BROWN, 4 STRANDS, Z-SPIN, S-PLY, 4 SHOOTS

PILE:        WOOL, 2 STRANDS, Z-SPIN, S-PLY

KNOT:       GHIORDES, ca. 48/inch

EDGES:      FLAT, DARK BROWN

ENDS:        KILIM WITH FRINGE; KILIM FOLDED AND SEWN

PREVIOUSLY PUBLISHED: Caucasian Rugs of Yesterday (Fokker)

## PLATE 5: **KARS**

4'4" x 10'8"

Dated 1929 and Inscribed
INSCRIPTION: **1929 TIV.IN / +ASBARMA**

Both the design and color of this rug show the influence Kurdish weaving has had in northeastern Turkey. The pattern is stark, the coloring simple, the pile thick. Like many older rugs from Turkey, this rug has been subjected to a certain amount of chemical fading. The heavy bleaching of semi-antique rugs was customary in the Turkish rug trade until quite recently.

A late example, this rug is stricter and more symmetrical than many similar weaves. Only the meticulous shaping of the letters and numbers in the description, and the few separate motifs scattered randomly in the field, betray the individuality of the weaver. ASBAR means a shield or a defence; the cross in the inscription implies a death.

PLATE 5

KARS   4'4" x 10'8"
Dated 1929 and Inscribed

COLORS:  Rose red, dark blue, gold, ivory, aniline purple, orange.

WARP:     WOOL, TAN AND BROWN, 3 STRANDS, Z-SPIN, S-PLY

WEFT:     WOOL, PURPLE, 2 STRANDS, Z-SPIN, S-PLY, 3-SHOOTS

PILE:     WOOL, 2 STRANDS, Z-SPIN, S-PLY

KNOT:     GHIORDES, ca. 56/inch

EDGES:    FLAT, DARK BROWN

ENDS:     KILIM FOLDED AND SEWN; KILIM AND FRINGE

PLATE 6: **KARS**

4'6" x 8'3"

Dated 1934 and Inscribed
INSCRIPTION: **61 1934 TIV ASHRAGHIS**
**61 1934 TIV TSERVANTGHOGH**

This brilliant rug was even more colorful before the aniline blue and purple medallions faded. The contrast of gold, aubergine and coral is well loved in the Kars region. Note the medallion-enclosed crosses on either side of the central row of medallions. Also typically Armenian are the pairs of confronted birds, in this case falcons. The falcon is a common motif in Armenian stone-carving as well as in rug design.

This rug is a late example of an old tradition, similar to the so-called "small-pattern Holbein" of four hundred years ago. It has become the custom among many writers on Oriental Rugs to use terms related to renaissance painters in describing rug patterns, since our earliest visual record of rugs imported to Europe lies in such works.

PLATE 6

**KARS**   4'6" x 8'3"
Dated 1934 and Inscribed

COLORS:   Purple, coral, gold, yellow, celedon, tan, ivory, aniline blue and purple.

WARP:   WOOL, TAN AND BROWN, 3 STRANDS, Z-SPIN, S-PLY

WEFT:   WOOL, TAN, 2 STRANDS, Z-SPIN, S-PLY, 2 SHOOTS

PILE:   WOOL, 2 STRANDS, Z-SPIN, S-PLY

KNOT:   GHIORDES, ca. 54/inch

EDGES:   FLAT, DARK BROWN

ENDS:   PLAIT WITH FRINGE

## PLATE 7: **DIYARBEKIR**

3'8" x 14'5"

Dated 1912, 1914 and Inscribed
INSCRIPTION: **1912**
                **1914 N'SHAN**

A classic tribal type of rug, from the vicinity of Diyabekir. Most such rugs are the work of the Yuruk people, Kurdish nomads in the area. In the days of historic Armenia, this was the site of Tigranakerta, the city of the Armenian Emperor. Since those days there has been a continuing Armenian presence.

After two medallions had been completed, the weaver dated the rug 1912, in very florid script. Two years passed before the third medallion was completed and the date 1914 added, along with the name of the weaver. It is possible that the entire rug was not completed until sometime in the 1920's.

PLATE 7

## DIYARBEKIR   3'8" x 14'5"
Dated 1912, 1914 and Inscribed

COLORS:  Red, dark blue, dark green, black, white, ivory, orange, coral, maroon.

WARP:    WOOL, NATURAL, 2 STRANDS, Z-SPIN, S-PLY

WEFT:    WOOL, DARK RED AND MAROON, 1 STRAND, Z-SPIN, S-PLY,
         3 SHOOTS

PILE:    WOOL, 2 STRANDS, Z-SPIN, S-PLY

KNOT:    GHIORDES, ca. 35/inch

EDGES:   FLAT, MULTI-COLOR

ENDS:    KILIM WITH PLAITED FRINGE

## PLATE 8: **DIYARBEKIR**

*4' x 8'6"*

Dated 1938 and Inscribed
INSCRIPTION: **1938 B V B** (upside down)

Another charming and irregular tribal type of rug, similar to the weavings of the Kurdish Yuruk people. The prominent date in the corner would not be enough to mark this rug as Armenian, since Turkish rugs have often been dated in western style since the reforms of Ataturk, a few years prior to the completion of this example.

In this rug however, we also find Armenian letters in the field at the end near the inscription. Also, there are the bird and animal motifs we asssociate with Armenian weaving in the center of the design, between the wildly mismatched medallions.

PLATE 8

DIYARBEKIR   4' x 8'6"
Dated 1938 and Inscribed

COLORS:  Henna, orange, green, ivory, black, aniline blue.

WARP:     WOOL, TAN AND IVORY, 3 STRANDS, Z-SPIN, S-PLY

WEFT:     WOOL, RED, 2 STRANDS, Z-SPIN, S-PLY, 1 SHOOT

PILE:     WOOL, 2 STRANDS, Z-SPIN, S-PLY

KNOT:     GHIORDES, 35/inch

EDGES:    FLAT, RED 3 STRANDS

ENDS:     KILIM PLAITED; KILIM FRINGED

## PLATE 9: **VAN JEJIM**

5'4" x 10'3"

Dated 1905 and Inscribed
INSCRIPTION: **1905**
                **THIS JEJIM WAS MADE BY**
                **DHA AND NMB, 1905**

This exquisite silk on cotton jejim was made in the vicinity of Van, one of the most renowned ancient Armenian cities. The wording of the inscription is typically "Vanetsi." Jejims — embroidered flat-weaves — are usually of wool or cotton and made for utilitarian purposes. They are not normally of silk, nor are they inscribed.

An extraordinary piece of workmanship such as this was not made in any casual manner. It must have been made as a gift, in commemoration of a wedding or birth or perhaps to adorn a church. The tile-like nature of the design, with many small diamonds forming a pattern of large diamonds, is architectural and helps support this last possibility. But whatever its purpose, we may be grateful that this fragile textile survived the horrors which so closely followed on its creation.

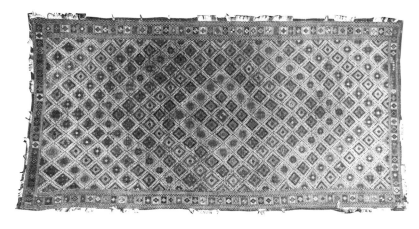

PLATE 9

VAN JEJIM 5'4" x 10'3"
Dated 1905 and Inscribed

SILK EMBROIDERY: Henna, straw yellow, apple green, ivory, rose pink, purple, coral.

WARP AND WEFT: INDIGO-DYED COTTON

EDGES AND ENDS: MULTI-COLORED SILK TASSEL OVER KILIM FOLDED AND SEWN

PREVIOUSLY PUBLISHED: The Gregorian Collection of Armenian Rugs (Dartmouth); Armenian Rugs — The Gregorian Collection (Michigan)

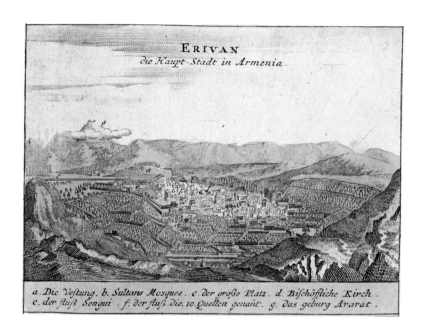

**ERIVAN The Capital of Armenia**

a view by Johann Baptist Homann    Nurnberg, 17th century

Another view in Homann's work shows Kars as the "largest Armenian
city." Erivan though smaller is called the capital because it is the center
of east Armenia and site of the Holy Mother Church. The rugs in the
following pages were probably woven within 100 km of Erivan, with
the exception of those from Gendje, further east.

## II: ARMENIAN RUGS OF THE CAUCASUS

The majority of rugs we know as Kazak come from the region of Lake Sevan, 80 km east of Erivan. Lori-Pembak is to the north, Karachoph is near the lake, Gendje lies a little further to the southeast. For western lovers of the Oriental Rug, the name Kazak is so firmly fixed to this class of rugs it is unlikely the nomenclature will ever change. The rugs actually made by the Kazakh people are shaggier, bolder and more Asiatic than the rugs made in Armenia and Georgia, and these authentic "Kazakhs" are not often seen on the market.

The Armenian Kazak tends to be simple in pattern. Often only a few colors are used, giving an effect of rich, subdued brilliance. Inscriptions are usually limited: the date, a few initials. These rugs seem to have changed little over the years: examples dated well into the twentieth century preserve old-fashioned simplicity and a timeless sense of color and design.

The first example is a Karachoph (Plate 10) typically square in proportion. Very little white is used. In Plates 12 and 13 the same outline has been stretched into a rectangle, creating a pattern that has been linked to the classic floor-plan of the Armenian church. Dr. Der Manuelian has suggested that just as in early times a church building might have been dedicated to the memory of a deceased person by a wealthy patron, in more recent times both the memorial steles called "khatchk'ar" and inscribed rugs laid out in a similar way may have fulfilled the same function.

Plates 14 and 15 are affecting in that they use no white at all: just the basic rich reds, blues and greens of Armenian manuscript painting. Plates 16 and 17 are of a style that has been associated with Lori-Pembak. The latter with its dates of 1919 and 1938 is an effective reminder of the great upheaval caused by war and massacre. The person who completed the rug was not the one who started it. Seven three-medallion Kazaks and a classic "Akstafa" (Plate 25) complete this group of classic square or broadly rectangular Kazaks.

Six 'long rugs' from the Gendje region are also included (Plates 26-31). The oldest dates from 1858, and was buried during the First World War for safe-keeping. This was a relatively common fate for Armenian household possessions, especially rugs, copper and brass-ware. Several rugs in our collection show signs of having been rudely preserved in this manner.

## PLATE 10: **KARACHOPH KAZAK**

6'10" x 8'

Dated 1913 and Inscribed
INSCRIPTION: **1913 TIV T.A.**

Karachoph is situated near Lake Sevan in Armenia. The name of this village has been applied to those Kazaks distinguished by square proportions and the use of four small corner medallions to balance a large square or cruciform central one. The design of this medallion suggests the floor-plan of a traditional Armenian church; such churches are in some cases more than 1000 years old.

In this example the use of color is rich but restrained and the design achieves rare elegance. Rugs of this vintage were the last of their kind to be woven in the Caucasus. World War I and its consequent tragedies brought an end to the classic period of rug creation.

PLATE 10

## KARACHOPH KAZAK   6'10" x 8'
Dated 1913 and Inscribed

COLORS:  Henna, midnight and medium blue, dark green, orange, ivory, black.

WARP:    WOOL, IVORY*

WEFT:    WOOL*

PILE:    WOOL*

KNOT:    GHIORDES, ca. 42/inch

EDGES:   FLAT, RED

ENDS:    KILIM UNRAVELLED; UNRAVELLED

*Rug unavailable for technical analysis
  Donated to the Armenian Library and Museum of America

## PLATE 11: **KAZAK**

5' x 6'7"

Dated 191? and Inscribed
INSCRIPTION: **191 T.T.** (garbled)

This is a primitive Armenian Kazak similar in proportion and motif to the classic "Karachoph," but lacking the small corner medallions. The cross-shaped finials on both the inner and outer medallions is a typical Armenian design and can be seen in other rugs in this collection, for example Plate 3 above. This is also a motif seen in Armenian stone-carving, on churches and on the memorial steles called "Khatchk'ar."

In this example, the weaver did not plan for the size of the central medallion when she started; she was forced to widen the red part and decrease the blue, giving the finished rug a lop-sided bulge and considerable charm. The emptiness of the field is effective and in Armenian weaving, relatively unusual.

PLATE 11

KAZAK   5' x 6'7"
Dated 191? and Inscribed

COLORS:   Henna, light blue, dark blue, ivory, dark brown, orange, gold, black.

WARP:   WOOL, NATURAL AND TAN, 3 STRANDS, Z-SPIN, S-PLY

WEFT:   WOOL, BROWN, 3 STRANDS, Z-SPIN, S-PLY, 2 SHOOTS

PILE:   WOOL, 2 STRANDS, Z-SPIN, S-PLY

KNOT:   GHIORDES, 56/INCH

EDGES:   FLAT, DARK BROWN

ENDS:   KILIM WITH PLAIT; FRINGED

## PLATE 12: **KAZAK** "KHATCHK'AR DESIGN"

4'4" x 7'

Dated 1919
INSCRIPTION: **1919 TIV / 1329**
                       (both dates reversed)

In this rug and the one following, the cruciform field has been elongated enough to
suggest comparison with the Khatchk'ar, a traditional Armenian cross carved in stone
and often inscribed as a memorial. The Khatchk'ar may be free-standing or built into the
wall of a church. It is commissioned and carved as a memorial and bears an inscription to
that effect.

Although there are corner medallions balancing the central one as in Karachoph Kazaks,
the longer proportion and deep-colored unadorned field create an altogether different and
more sober effect. This sombre rug, reflective of a sombre period in Armenian history is
clearly commemorative in feeling. The date is recorded in Islamic form balancing the
Armenian script. There are some elderly Armenians who remember rugs of this design
and hue being woven as memorials. It may have been a less expensive alternative to the
commissioning of a Khatchk'ar in stone, and one which had the added advantage of being
portable.

PLATE 12

## KAZAK "KHATCHK'AR DESIGN"   4'4" x 7'
Dated 1919

COLORS: Henna, dark and light blue, medium green, dark brown, ivory.

WARP:    WOOL, BROWN AND IVORY, 3 STRANDS, Z-SPIN, S-PLY

WEFT:    WOOL, BROWN, 2 STRANDS, Z-SPIN, S-PLY, 2 SHOOTS

PILE:    WOOL, 2 STRANDS, Z-SPIN, S-PLY

KNOT:    GHIORDES, ca. 56/inch

EDGES:   FLAT, RED-BROWN

ENDS:    KILIM WITH PLAIT; UNRAVELLED

PREVIOUSLY PUBLISHED: Armenian Rugs — The Gregorian Collection (Michigan)

## PLATE 13: **KAZAK** "KHATCHK'AR DESIGN"

*4'9" x 8'4"*

Dated Oct. 2, 1912
INSCRIPTION: **1912.2.10 AMI/ 1332**

Clearly this rug is commemorative, since it is precisely dated 2-10-1912. It is relatively uncommon for an Armenian rug to show the date in Islamic as well as in Armenian form, but both this rug and the preceding, similar example do so. Once again the field is outlined in stylized cruciform shape. Once again the corner medallions and their central balance (in this case three small medallions) are secondary to the strongly outlined shape of the field.

To one side of the center a saddle horse with the high tail-carriage of an Arabian is shown, with another partially completed below the upper Islamic date. There is also a garbled form of the date and several false starts of either dates, inscriptions, or animals. The empty-saddled horse may well symbolize the death of a male family member.

PLATE 13

KAZAK "KHATCHK'AR DESIGN"   4'9" x 8'4"
Dated Oct. 2, 1912

COLORS:   Henna, dark and medium blue, madder, dark and light brown, ivory, yellow.

WARP:      WOOL, TAN AND IVORY, 2 STRANDS, Z-SPIN, S-PLY

WEFT:      WOOL, TAN AND RED, 2 STRANDS, Z-SPIN, S-PLY, 1-3 SHOOTS

PILE:       WOOL, 2 STRANDS, Z-SPIN, S-PLY

KNOT:      GHIORDES, ca. 64/inch

EDGES:    FLAT, RED

ENDS:      1" BRAIDED; KILIM

PREVIOUSLY PUBLISHED: Weavers, Merchants and Kings (Fort Worth)

## PLATE 14: **KAZAK** "EREBUNI DESIGN"

4'9" x 7'3"

Dated 1886 (?)

Erebuni is an ancient name for modern Yerevan, and rugs of this classic type seem to have been made in this district, today the capital of Soviet Armenia. A deep, rich, sombre range of color and a relatively thick pile characterize these rugs.

The simple colors of this example are the favorites of classic Armenian manuscript illumination and early Armenian architectural decoration. The lack of any light color or even a touch of white is as impressive as it is unusual. White is always available, in the form of undyed wool or cotton, so its exclusion is a matter of deliberate aesthetic choice. It is interesting to consider that in a relatively small region like the Caucasus a relatively small group of people like the Armenians could have a rug-weaving tradition embracing styles as diverse as this simple five-colored rug (two of the colors being undyed brown and tan) and the very busy rug in Plate 77 below, with sixteen colors.

PLATE 14

KAZAK "EREBUNI DESIGN"    4'9" x 7'3"
Dated 1886 (?)

COLORS:  Henna, abrashed medium blue, light green, natural tan, natural dark brown.

WARP:      WOOL, BROWN AND TAN, 3 STRANDS, Z-SPIN, S-PLY

WEFT:       WOOL, BROWN AND RED, 2 STRANDS, Z-SPIN, S-PLY, 3 SHOOTS

PILE:        WOOL, 2 STRANDS, Z-SPIN, S-PLY

KNOT:       GHIORDES, ca. 42/INCH

EDGES:      FLAT, RED

ENDS:       KILIM WITH PLAITED FRINGE; KILIM WITH FRINGE

## PLATE 15: **KAZAK**

4′4″ x 6′8″

Dated Nov. 7, 1927 and Inscribed
INSCRIPTION:  **19 11/7 27 TVIN MANEAG**

This is a late example of the tradition exemplified by the preceding rug. The rich, thick pile and simple range of colors are still in evidence, but the design has become more complex. It appears to be a simplification, redrawn on a larger scale, of the type of design used in the medallions of certain classic Karabagh rugs, e.g. Plate 40 below.

The curving leaf-shapes with serrated edges carry a suggestion of the ancient Armenian *VISHAP* or dragon motif, seen in many *VISHAPAGORG* (dragon-rug) designs below. In a rug this late such a borrowing is likely to be deliberate, rather than spontaneous.

PLATE 15

KAZAK   4'4" x 6'8"
Dated Nov. 7, 1927 and Inscribed

COLORS:  Henna, abrashed blue, dark green, dark brown.

WARP:     WOOL, BROWN AND NATURAL, 3 STRANDS, Z-SPIN, S-PLY

WEFT:      WOOL, BROWN, 2 STRANDS, Z-SPIN, S-PLY, 2 SHOOTS

PILE:        WOOL, 2 STRANDS, Z-SPIN, S-PLY

KNOT:      GHIORDES, 48

EDGES:     FLAT, DARK BROWN

ENDS:       KILIM WITH FRINGE; FRINGE

PLATE 16 : **LORI PEMBAK KAZAK**
4′6″ x 7′5″   Dated 1919, 1938
INSCRIPTION: **1919** (in field)
                          **1938** (in border, reversed)


PLATE 17: **LORI PEMBAK KAZAK**
4′ x 10′   Dated 1914 and Inscribed
INSCRIPTION: **1914 TIV PEL**

These rugs exemplify the hard-edged stylization and crisp colors we associate with Lori Pembak, a region of north Armenia. The Lori Pembak typically is rectangular, with a lozenge-shaped medallion and tooth-edged field separated by a secondary narrow field. The rug in Plate 16 was left incomplete by the weaver. The date 1919 is worked into the upper right-hand side of the field; about 12″ above this date, the wool, dyes and style of knotting change. The upper border is dated 1938 in a more careful manner than the earlier inscription. Presumably the original weaver was a victim of the upheavals and tragedies which followed the First World War.

It is interesting to compare the above rug with Plate 17. This is a dignified rug with glowing colors and a heavy, velvet nap. There are many repetitions of the Armenian letter 'd', thought by some to be decorative shorthand for Der, 'the Lord'. Flowering plants ranged on either side of the central lozenge are stacked to make a tree-of-life motif.

PLATE 16                                    PLATE 17

## PLATE 16: LORI PEMBAK KAZAK   4'6" x 7'5"
Dated 1919, 1938

COLORS:  Magenta, henna, orange, gold, dark and medium blue, ivory, black.

WARP:     WOOL, BROWN AND NATURAL, 3 STRANDS, Z-SPIN, S-PLY

WEFT:     WOOL, DARK RED, 2 STRANDS, Z-SPIN, S-PLY, 2 SHOOTS

PILE:     WOOL, 2 STRANDS, Z-SPIN, S-PLY

KNOT:     GHIORDES, ca. 36/inch

EDGES:    NOT ORIGINAL     ENDS:     UNRAVELLED


## PLATE 17: LORI PEMBAK KAZAK   4' x 10'
Dated 1914 and Inscribed

COLORS:  Red, chestnut, orange, dark blue, dark and light green, yellow, tan, black,
ivory, aniline purple

WARP:     WOOL, TAN, 3 STRANDS, Z-SPIN, S-PLY

WEFT:     WOOL, NATURAL AND BROWN, 2 STRANDS, Z-SPIN, S-PLY, 2 SHOOTS

PILE:     WOOL, 2 STRANDS, Z-SPIN, S-PLY

KNOT:     GHIORDES, ca. 56/inch

EDGES:    FLAT, BLACK     ENDS:     KILIM FOLDED AND SEWN

## PLATE 18: **KAZAK** "THREE MEDALLION DESIGN"

4'10" x 7'10"

Dated 1929
INSCRIPTION: **19299**
            **1929 1929**

It is interesting to compare this simple three-medallion Kazak, woven in 1929, with
the child-like pictorial of a Soviet soldier on horseback woven the same year (Plate 86).
Despite the late and politically troubled date of weaving, each rug uses one of the earliest
and most basic of motifs, the tree of life. Pairs of birds adorn the pictorial rug; there is a
single bird atop the upper central tree in this one.

In the Sixth Century A.D., an anonymous Armenian monk wrote:
        A little bird I saw — a peerless one
        Upon the four-armed sign, that peer hath none.
        O Peerless One, who is like Thee,
        Thou Peerless One.
        Thou alone.
Birds in trees had been a traditional part of pre-Christian Armenian art; to symbolize
Christ on the cross with a bird on a tree was an easy and logical step. It is likely that this
graphic symbol was made even more popular by the Armenian folk-belief in the souls of
the deceased appearing as birds.

PLATE 18

KAZAK "THREE MEDALLION DESIGN"    4'10" x 7'10"
Dated 1929

COLORS:  Henna, dark and light blue, medium green, gold, dark brown, ivory.

WARP:    WOOL, NATURAL, 3 STRANDS, Z-SPIN, S-PLY

WEFT:    WOOL, RED, 2 STRANDS, Z-SPIN, S-PLY, 2 SHOOTS

PILE:    WOOL, 2 STRANDS, Z-SPIN, S-PLY

KNOT:    GHIORDES, ca. 60/inch

EDGES:   FLAT, RED

ENDS:    PLAITED FRINGE; UNRAVELLED

PLATE 19: **KAZAK** "THREE MEDALLION DESIGN"

5'1" x 7'

Dated 1909 and Inscribed
INSCRIPTION: **MAGART 1909**
                **GIALA (?) AGH REG MAGART**

This classic three-medallion Kazak probably was inscribed to commemorate a sacrament since *agh*, salt, is a reference to baptism. The inscriptions on the left-hand side are much more tentative than those on the right. Traditional motifs such as bold crosses and confronted pairs of birds are also present, and the strong tones of blue, green and red are typical of central Armenian weaving.

This rug is a good example of opportunistic inscription, that is, a rug already on the loom receiving commemorative notations. It does not seem to have been woven for the purpose of bearing its inscription.

PLATE 19

KAZAK "THREE MEDALLION DESIGN"   5'1" x 7'
Dated 1909 and Inscribed

COLORS:  Henna, dark blue, gold, yellow, dark and light green, dark brown, ivory,
orange.

WARP:     WOOL, NATURAL, 3 STRANDS, Z-SPIN, S-PLY

WEFT:     WOOL, RED, 2 STRANDS, Z-SPIN, S-PLY, 3 SHOOTS

PILE:     WOOL, 2 STRANDS, Z-SPIN, S-PLY

KNOT:     GHIORDES, ca. 42/inch

EDGES:    FLAT, RED

ENDS:     KILIM WITH PLAIT, UNRAVELLED

PLATE 20: **KAZAK** "THREE MEDALLION DESIGN"

*5'9" x 7'7"*

Dated 1904
INSCRIPTION: **1904 AMI**

This rug is similar to the preceding one, but less adventuresome in color and design. The motif in the main border is strongly cruciform and among the random elements scattered in the field there is, in the middle right, an equilateral cross enclosed within a small stepped medallion. There is an appealing childishness about the number of incomplete or enigmatic motifs that fill this rug: the overall artistic effect is of a sampler or an experiment.

PLATE 20

KAZAK "THREE MEDALLION DESIGN"    5'9" x 7'7"
Dated 1904

COLORS:  Henna, dark blue, medium green, gold, dark brown, ivory.

WARP:    WOOL, IVORY AND TAN, 2 STRANDS, Z-SPIN, S-PLY

WEFT:    WOOL, RED, 2 STRANDS, Z-SPIN, S-PLY, 3-4 SHOOTS

PILE:    WOOL, 2 STRANDS, Z-SPIN, S-PLY

KNOT:    GHIORDES, ca. 48/inch

EDGES:   FLAT, RED

ENDS:    KILIM WITH PLAIT

## PLATE 21: **KAZAK** "THREE MEDALLION DESIGN"

5'11" x 9'

Dated 1911 and Inscribed
INSCRIPTION: **ASAK P.**
 **ARP. 1911 TIV**

Another classic Kazak, extremely regular and straight forward. The weaver has permitted herself only a little free expression, by including a confronted pair of crested birds in the first medallion. As with most rugs of this tradition, the color balance is superb.

It is likely that this rug commemorates a wedding. The cryptic inscription names a man and a woman, Asak and Arpen; the greek 'P' which follows Asak's name is the initial letter of the Armenian word for bridegroom.

PLATE 21

KAZAK "THREE MEDALLION DESIGN"   5'11" x 9'
Dated 1911 and Inscribed

COLORS:   Henna, dark blue, green, yellow, dark and light brown, ivory.

WARP:      WOOL, IVORY, 2 STRANDS, Z-SPIN, S-PLY

WEFT:       WOOL, RED, 2 STRANDS, Z-SPIN, S-PLY, 2-3 SHOOTS

PILE:         WOOL, 2 STRANDS, Z-SPIN, S-PLY

KNOT:       GHIORDES, ca. 63/INCH

EDGES:     FLAT, LIGHT BROWN

ENDS:       KILIM FOLDED AND SEWN; UNRAVELLED

PREVIOUSLY PUBLISHED: Weavers, Merchants and Kings (Fort Worth)

PLATE 22: **KAZAK** "MODIFIED THREE-MEDALLION"

4'8" x 7'11"

Dated Mar 20, 1911 and Inscribed
INSCRIPTION: **1911 KANVIOV MARD 20 IN**

The weaver of this rug intended a classic three-medallion design; above the third
medallion there is a clear demarcation, a line of abrash across the henna-colored field
where the design was planned to change to a final border. For some reason, apparently
commemorative, another small medallion was added supporting an inscription above it.
This extra medallion was based on one of the rug's subsidiary designs, not on one of its
three major central medallions.

The change of design in this rug is all the more remarkable when one considers its strictly
symmetrical nature, its lack of personal touches or whimsy. The exact nature of the date
implies a commemorative purpose.

PLATE 22

PLATE 22

## KAZAK   4'8" x 7'11"
Dated Mar 20, 1911 and Inscribed

COLORS:  Henna, red-brown, brown, ivory, tan, teal blue, medium pink, yellow.

WARP:    WOOL, GREY, BROWN, IVORY 3 STRANDS, Z-SPIN, S-PLY

WEFT:    WOOL, BLUE, 2 STRANDS, Z-SPIN, S-PLY, 3 SHOOTS

PILE:    WOOL, 2 STRANDS, Z-SPIN, S-PLY

KNOT:    GHIORDES, 56/inch

EDGES:   ROUND BROWN

ENDS:    BLUE KILIM AND BRAID; UNRAVELLED

PLATE 23: **KAZAK** "THREE MEDALLION DESIGN"

4'6" x 6'10"

Dated 1914 and Inscribed
INSCRIPTION: **1914 VSLI. AGH. 1914** (?)  **OV**

The deep brown field is usually an indication of Azerbaijani influence; although this is clearly a Kazak it has elements that relate to the region south of the Arax river. The inscription, badly worn, seems to refer to a sacrament (*agh,* salt,) involving someone named Vasili in 1914. Another religious note is struck by the clearly delineated orb and cross, woven in bright pink to the left of the first medallion. Many spirited human figures and animals are scattered through the field, including a confronted pair of birds. This rug appears to have suffered a crude attempt at obliterating its inscription.

It is interesting to compare this spontaneous creation with the attractive, precise, somewhat cold rug preceding (Plate 22). Each is a three-medallion Kazak, with a commemorative inscription across the top of the field; the preceding rug is dated 1911 and this one 1914. Yet the two are worlds apart, and the 1911 rug seems later than the 1914 example, in that it is more perfect and less personal. It is a good reminder that rugs vary more from weaver to weaver than they do from year to year; one weaver may well make a rug of a certain type over and over again, during a lifespan of many decades.

PLATE 23

## KAZAK "THREE MEDALLION DESIGN"   4'6" x 6'10"
Dated 1914 and Inscribed

COLORS:  Henna, orange, gold, yellow, rose, dark blue, green, dark brown, natural tan,
              ivory, aniline bright pink.

WARP:     WOOL, BROWN AND TAN, 3 STRANDS, Z-SPIN, S-PLY

WEFT:      WOOL, BROWN, 2 STRANDS, Z-SPIN, S-PLY, 2 SHOOTS

PILE:       WOOL, 2 STRANDS, Z-SPIN, S-PLY

KNOT:     GHIORDES, ca. 56/inch

EDGES:    FLAT, MULTI-COLOR

ENDS:     UNRAVELLED

PREVIOUSLY PUBLISHED: The Gregorian Collection of Armenian Rugs (Dartmouth);
Armenian Rugs — The Gregorian Collection (Michigan)

## PLATE 24: **KAZAK** "THREE MEDALLION DESIGN"

4' x 8'

Dated 1907 and Inscribed
INSCRIPTION: (Handwritten on left; unclear)
**1907 TIV**

This charming rug appears to commemorate an important family event, possibly a wedding or the safe return of a son from the army. The figure of a soldier is woven in duplicate above the central medallion, and below the same medallion a couple holding hands is similarly depicted. The man wears a long white coat, like a shepherd, over a tunic with buttons. The woman has a bright red hat with a white scarf over it.

One of the soldier figures touches an equilateral cross with his hand, so possibly there was a son who did not return. The rest of the field is filled with animals, birds, and small medallions. The motif filling the medallions is more typical of Karabagh weaving than of Kazak.

PLATE 24

# KAZAK "THREE MEDALLION DESIGN"   4' x 8'
Dated 1907 and Inscribed

COLORS:  Henna, tan, dark brown, ivory, dark blue, gold, yellow, coral.

WARP:    WOOL, NATURAL, 3 STRANDS, Z-SPIN, S-PLY

WEFT:    WOOL, ORANGE AND NATURAL, 3 STRANDS, Z-SPIN, S-PLY,
         2 SHOOTS

PILE:    WOOL, 2 STRANDS, Z-SPIN, S-PLY

KNOT:    GHIORDES, 63/inch

EDGES:   FLAT, ORANGE

ENDS:    KILIM WITH PLAITED BAND

## PLATE 25: **KAZAK** "AKSTAFA DESIGN"

4'10" x 6'5"

Dated 1915
INSCRIPTION: **1915 TIV**

"Akstafa" is the name given to a design of eight-sided medallions flanked by stylized peacocks. "Akstafa" rugs are woven in many parts of the Caucasus, and variations of this design are common in the northern Persian towns of Ardebil and Meshkin.

The stylization and simplicity of this rug suggest a link with the Azerbaijan, even though the weave is clearly Kazak. Note how the main motif within the medallions is made to form an equilateral cross, the ends of which are diamond-tipped, an ancient Armenian design. A part of this rug's subtle beauty lies in its apparent regularity, concealing a high degree of eccentricity only noticeable upon a closer, second look.

PLATE 25

KAZAK "AKSTAFA DESIGN"   4'10" x 6'5"
Dated 1915

COLORS:  Red, dark blue, yellow, green, dark and light brown, ivory.

WARP:     WOOL, TAN, 2 STRANDS, Z-SPIN, S-PLY

WEFT:     WOOL, BROWN, 2 STRANDS, Z-SPIN, S-PLY, 2 SHOOTS

PILE:      WOOL, 2 STRANDS, Z-SPIN, S-PLY

KNOT:     GHIORDES, ca. 64/inch

EDGES:    FLAT, RED-BROWN

ENDS:     BLUE/BROWN STRIPES AND A PLAITED BAND; DARK BROWN KILIM

PREVIOUSLY PUBLISHED: The Gregorian Collection Of Armenian Rugs (Dartmouth);
Weavers, Merchants and Kings (Fort Worth); Armenian Rugs — The Gregorian
Collection (Michigan)

## PLATE 26: **GENDJE** "NOUSH DESIGN"

4'3" x 10'3"

Dated 1881
INSCRIPTION: **1881 AMI** (woven upside down)

We bought this rug from an Armenian family resident in Turkey, which had buried its valuables for safe-keeping during the period of massacres. The rug was in the ground more than four years, yet it has remained strong, glossy and supple. The damage is from vermin. This is a fine example of the classic long rug of the Gendje district, diagonally banded with a simple large-scale pattern.

In the pages following we have chosen to call this design "noush," the Armenian term, rather than use the Persian term "boteh" or the European term "paisley." Whether used on a large scale, as here, or on a small scale, e.g. Plate 52, the "noush" motif is a familiar one in the textile arts of the Middle East.

PLATE 26

GENDJE "NOUSH DESIGN"   4'3" x 10'3"
Dated 1881

COLORS:  Henna, dark blue, green, mustard, dark brown, ivory.

WARP:     WOOL, BROWN AND TAN, 3 STRANDS, Z-SPIN, S-PLY

WEFT:      WOOL, BROWN, 2 STRANDS, Z-SPIN, S-PLY, 2 SHOOTS

PILE:        WOOL, 2 STRANDS, Z-SPIN, S-PLY

KNOT:      GHIORDES, ca. 36/inch

EDGES:     FLAT, LIGHT BLUE

ENDS:       KILIM PLAITED; UNRAVELLED

PREVIOUSLY PUBLISHED: Armenian Rugs — The Gregorian Collection (Michigan)

## PLATE 27: **GENDJE**

3'10" x 12'

Dated 1858 and Inscribed
INSCRIPTION: (a long inscription, apparently religious)

This dignified rug exemplifies the use of Christian symbolism in Armenian rug-weaving. The central medallions and the repeated border motif are each composed of stylized, ornate crosses. The effect is architectural, giving the impression of glazed tile. It is likely that this rug was especially woven for use at the altar in an Armenian church.

The rugs shown in Plates 26-30 are all Kazaks, of the type commonly classified as Gendje. This family of Caucasian weaving is noted for its long, narrow proprotions, relatively fine weave, use of repetitive design motifs and flat, sometimes multi-colored edges.

Other Armenian-inscribed rugs using repetitive tile motifs are known, usually of the Karabagh type. Plate 56 below is one example.

PLATE 27

GENDJE   3'10" x 12
Dated 1858 and Inscribed

COLORS:  Red, rose, dark and medium blue, dark green, gold, ivory, black.

WARP:    WOOL, IVORY*

WEFT:    WOOL*

PILE:    WOOL*

KNOT:    GHIORDES, ca. 81/inch

EDGES:   FLAT, MULTI-COLOR

ENDS:    UNRAVELLED

*Rug unavailable for analysis
 Donated to the Armenian Library and Museum of America

PLATE 28: **GENDJE** "GUL DESIGN"

3'10" x 8'3"

Dated 1888 and Inscribed
INSCRIPTION: **AGH. NOUBAR GRIGOR BAGHD'S'I'NTS**
**IN 1888**
**SHARIAN IN 1888**

This is a rug of extraordinary beauty and interest, in an extraordinary state of preservation. The word *agh*, salt, implies some important sacrament is being commemorated, a birth or marriage. The inclusion of the inscription in the side borders half-way along the length of the rug shows that this rug was woven as a commemorative.

Since the Gendje area adjoins the regions of Karabagh, Shirvan and traditional Kazak territories, it is not surprising that many classic Caucasian elements are present in the borders. The pairs of animals, in this case goats, are typically Armenian. The use of the 'stepped gul' design, as common to Central Asia as to the Caucasus, and the brilliance of the warm colors give the rug an almost Asiatic flavor.

PLATE 28

GENDJE "GUL DESIGN"  3'10" x 8'3"
Dated 1888 and Inscribed

COLORS:  Magenta, henna, gold, medium and light blue, green, pink, black, ivory.

WARP:  WOOL, IVORY AND TAN, 2 STRANDS, Z-SPIN, S-PLY

WEFT:  WOOL, IVORY, 2 STRANDS, Z-SPIN, S-PLY, 2 SHOOTS

PILE:  WOOL, Z-SPIN, S-PLY

KNOT:  GHIORDES, ca. 81/inch

EDGES:  FLAT, MULTI-COLOR

ENDS:  KILIM

PREVIOUSLY PUBLISHED: The Gregorian Collection Of Armenian Rugs (Dartmouth);
Armenian Rugs — The Gregorian Collection (Michigan); Weavers, Merchants and Kings
(Fort Worth)

PLATE 29: **GENDJE**
4'10" x 9'   Dated 1895 and Inscribed
INSCRIPTION: **1895 NARKIZ DER PARSIGHOV**

PLATE 30: **GENDJE** "LESHGI STAR DESIGN"
4'4" x 13'   Dated 1895
INSCRIPTION: **1895 AMI**

These rugs use different designs, but they share much more than the date of their completion. Technically, they are quite similar in construction and choice of colors. In each, the weaver has made the decision to leave the final medallion only half-done, in order to inscribe the rug and finish it. Each has many random, personal motifs filling the small amount of field left by the large central medallions.

In Plate 29, a man stands under a canopy half-way down the left-hand side of the field; below him the Armenian date monogram "AMI" appears in a column of small medallions. A modified naturalistic rose design forms the narrow guard borders, after the style of certain Karabagh rugs.

In Plate 30, there are several groups of animals and birds, as well as two pairs of human figures near the middle of the rug. Every other medallion has cross-shaped finials on the inside of the lateral arms of the design. Furthermore, the radiating diagonal arms of the motif are intensified by boxed arrowheads, a version of the design seen in Plate 3 above.

It is likely that each of these rugs was finished and dated in response to the political troubles of 1895. Plate 29 may be in memory of the individual named after the date.

PLATE 29

PLATE 30

## PLATE 29: GENDJE    4'10" x 9'
Dated 1895 and Inscribed

COLORS:   Henna, dark brown, tan, ivory, light blue, dark blue, yellow, light green, coral.

WARP:      WOOL, TAN, 3 STRANDS, Z-SPIN, S-PLY

WEFT:       WOOL, FADED ORANGE, 2 STRANDS, Z-SPIN, S-PLY, 2 SHOOTS

PILE:        WOOL, 2 STRANDS, Z-SPIN, S-PLY

KNOT:      GHIORDES, 63/inch

EDGES:    FLAT, MULTI-COLOR      ENDS:      FRAYED

## PLATE 30: GENDJE "LESHGI STAR DESIGN" 4'4" x 13'
Dated 1895

COLORS:   Henna, dark brown, ivory, light blue, dark blue, gold, orange.

WARP:      WOOL, NATURAL AND BROWN, 3 STRANDS, Z-SPIN, S-PLY

WEFT:       WOOL, BROWN, 3 STRANDS, Z-SPIN, S-PLY, 3 SHOOTS

PILE:        WOOL, 2 STRANDS, Z-SPIN, S-PLY

KNOT:      GHIORDES, 56/inch

EDGES:    FLAT, MULTI-COLOR     ENDS:    KILIM FOLDED AND SEWN (TWICE)

## PLATE 31: **GENDJE**

3'6" x 10'5"

ca. 1880, Inscribed
## INSCRIPTION: **GH R GH**

The long proportions and simple, repeated octagons would seem to suggest a rug from the eastern Caucasus, the Shirvan or Kuba district. The Gendje area is more likely, as a region known to be central to Armenian weaving. Although the color scheme is typical of many Armenian Kazaks, the over-all effect is much quieter. The weave is relatively close and fine, though not as fine as a typical rug from Kuba or Shirvan.

This rug is not as obviously Armenian as the preceding examples. It would be easy to overlook the small, ornate Armenian initials in the bottom medallion. Note the four tiny crosses in each medallion, and the central crosses in the three ivory medallions.

PLATE 31

PLATE 31

## GENDJE   3'6" x 10'5"
ca. 1880, Inscribed

COLORS: Henna, mauve, dark blue, yellow, dark brown, ivory.

WARP:     WOOL, NATURAL, 2 STRANDS, Z-SPIN, S-PLY

WEFT:     WOOL, BROWN, 2 STRANDS, Z-SPIN, S-PLY, 2 SHOOTS

PILE:     WOOL, 2 STRANDS, Z-SPIN, S-PLY

KNOT:     GHIORDES, ca. 56/inch

EDGES:    FLAT, DARK BROWN

ENDS:     UNRAVELLED

- 71 -

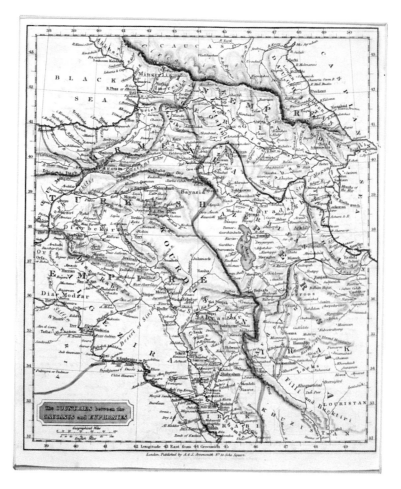

## The COUNTRIES between the CAUCASUS and EUPHRATES

English early 19th c.

On this map Armenia is shown crossing geopolitical boundries, arching from the Turkish Empire on the west to Persia on the east. The district of Karabagh is shown just east of Armenia's final 'a'. This fertile region is as rich in artistic expression as it is in crops: by far the greatest extant number of Armenian weavings come from Karabagh.

# III: ARMENIAN RUGS OF KARABAGH

The Arax river — "Mother Arax" in many Armenian poems — bisects the province of Azerbaijan, separating Iran from the Soviet Caucasus. On the southern, Iranian side, lie Karadagh and the Moghan district: on the northern bank are Karabagh and Nakhchevan. Karabagh was the pleasant region where Timur's massive army camped and refreshed itself during his Persian, Mesopotamian and Anatolian campaigns. The people we call "Azeri Turks" are locally named Tartar and are considered the descendants of Timur's army.

Despite Tartar encroachment, the majority of people living in Karabagh remained Armenian. Today, in the modern Soviet Union, Karabagh is part of the Soviet Azerbaijan and the abutting Armenian territory of Nakhchevan is a separate republic attached to the Soviet Azerbaijan. This was done deliberately to keep Armenian influence from becoming too concentrated in the Caucasus, and is still a point of grievance for some Armenians. The rugs in the following section bear dates ranging from 1810-1929; dated and initialled Armenian rugs are still being made in this region today. Nakhchevan and Shusha are two of the best-known towns in this region.

Rugs once known to the rug trade as "Dragon," "Cloudband" or "Eagle" Kazaks are now attributed to Karabagh. Armenians term all these patterns *Vishapagorg*, "dragon-carpet" and early forms of this classic and widely admired pattern can be found in the world's museums, though rarely are they attributed to Armenian weavers. The Armenian claim to have originated this pattern has been argued over the years in technical monographs. Of the forty-one rugs pictured below, more than one quarter show variations on this ancient theme.

A constant theme in all Armenian art is the confronted pair of birds, often atop a tree. In a classic *Vishapagorg* such as Plate 34, also our Cover Rug, one may easily see a variation on this theme, with rooster-like dragons, one dark, one light, in opposition. The tree which separates them has been reduced to an inverted 'v' terminating in stylized blossoms.

PLATE 32: **KARABAGH** *VISHAPAGORG* "CLOUDBAND DESIGN"
3'8" x 7'4"   Dated 1885 and Inscribed
INSCRIPTION: **TUMAR**+**TAKVIOV** + **1885 AMI**
          garbled letters


PLATE 33: **KARABAGH** *VISHAPAGORG* "CLOUDBAND DESIGN"
3'6" x 7'2"   Dated 1907 and Inscribed
INSCRIPTION: **1907 N.S.**

This classic Karabagh design was once called "cloudband" and until recently was considered a member of the Kazak family. So many inscribed Armenian examples have been located it seems to be a specifically Armenian type, although there are of course examples woven by other ethnic groups. It is one of a group of patterns known to Armenians as *Vishapagorg* (dragon-carpet). In a 'cloudband' rug the drawing of the *Vishap* (dragon) resembles a stylized rooster. They are always drawn in confronted pairs, dark and light. The inverted 'v' with blossoms which separates them seems to be the remnant of an earlier bush or tree motif. In this manner the 'cloudband' *Vishapagorg* recalls a classic motif of ancient Mesopotamia, two bird-headed gods facing each other on either side of a stylized tree which they are tending.

In Plate 32, the crosses in the inscription imply that the rug is a memorial to the person named. This dedicatory inscription is beautifully formed, unlike the crude, spontaneous letters in the field. In Plate 33, the idea to inscribe the rug apparently was made late: the weaver began the legs of two facing birds, then changed to date and initials. The condition suggests that this rug, like so many Armenian treasures, was buried at one time for safe-keeping. Despite the rotted holes and eaten edges the rug is fresh, strong and colorful.

PLATE 33

PLATE 32

## PLATE 32: KARABAGH *VISHAPAGORG*
###        "CLOUDBAND DESIGN"    3'8" x 7'4"
Dated 1885 and Inscribed

COLORS:  Henna, dark and abrashed medium blue, teal, gold, purple, ivory, black.

WARP:      WOOL, IVORY, 2 STRANDS, Z-SPIN, S-PLY

WEFT:      WOOL, TAN, 2 STRANDS, Z-SPIN, S-PLY, 2 SHOOTS

PILE:      WOOL, 2 STRANDS, Z-SPIN, S-PLY

KNOT:      GHIORDES, ca. 42/inch

EDGES:    FLAT, TAN          ENDS:  UNRAVELLED

## PLATE 33: KARABAGH *VISHAPAGORG*
###        "CLOUDBAND DESIGN"    3'6" x 7'2"
Dated 1907 and Inscribed

COLORS:  Red, henna, pink, gold, yellow, medium blue, medium green, tan, ivory, black.

WARP:      WOOL, BROWN AND NATURAL, 3 STRANDS, Z-SPIN, S-PLY

WEFT:      WOOL, CORAL, 2 STRANDS, Z-SPIN, S-PLY, 2 SHOOTS

PILE:      WOOL, 2 STRANDS, Z-SPIN, S-PLY

KNOT:      GHIORDES, ca. 48/inch

EDGES:    FLAT, MULTI-COLOR          ENDS:  KILIM FOLDED AND SEWN; KILIM FRINGED

PREVIOUSLY PUBLISHED: (32) Weavers, Merchants and Kings (Fort Worth);
(33) Armenian Rugs — The Gregorian Collection (Michigan); (32,33) The Gregorian
Collection Of Armenian Rugs (Dartmouth)

## PLATE 34: **KARABAGH** *VISHAPAGORG* "CLOUDBAND DESIGN"

4'3" x 7'10"

Dated 1898 and Inscribed
INSCRIPTION: **1898 A.A.**

This rug has been patched extensively through the center and part of the bottom edge is missing. It is likely that this rug also was buried at one time for safe-keeping. Tiny equilateral crosses fill in the medallions that are scattered throughout the field, but the main design is forcefully pre-Christian and archaic. As in Plate 32 above, the dark and light *Vishap* are placed in confronted pairs around a device equally ancient, the swastika or solar wheel.

It should be pointed out that much of the apparent difference in design between the top and bottom pairs of *Vishap* and the right and left pairs of *Vishap* is simply the result of construction technique. Rug designs which are square when laid out on a graph have a tendency in real life to become flattened as the weaver hammers the rows of knots into place. This physical fact, plus the constraints laid on the designer to fit them into a medallion of a certain shape, creates the difference. The color balance of this example is particularly noteworthy.

PLATE 34

KARABAGH *VISHAPAGORG* "CLOUDBAND DESIGN"   4'3" x 7'10"
Dated 1898 and Inscribed

COLORS:   Red, henna, coral, pink, gold, dark and medium blue, teal, green, ivory,
              dark brown.

WARP:   WOOL, TAN, 3 STRANDS, Z-SPIN, S-PLY

WEFT:   WOOL, NATURAL, 2 STRANDS, Z-SPIN, S-PLY, 2 SHOOTS

PILE:   WOOL, 2 STRANDS, Z-SPIN, S-PLY

KNOT:   GHIORDES, ca. 56/inch

EDGES:   FLAT, MULTI-COLOR

ENDS:   UNRAVELLED

PREVIOUSLY PUBLISHED: Armenian Rugs — The Gregorian Collection (Michigan)

This rug is also reproduced as our Cover Rug.

PLATE 35: **KARABAGH *VISHAPAGORG*** "CLOUDBAND DESIGN"
4'6" x 7'   Dated 1918 and Inscribed
INSCRIPTION: **1918** (letters garbled)


PLATE 36: **KARABAGH *VISHAPAGORG*** "CLOUDBAND DESIGN"
4' x 7'6"
UNINSCRIBED

Two more classic *Vishapagorg* of the 'cloudband' family. Plate 36, while uninscribed, is included because of its close stylistic and color links with the other inscribed examples. Its only unusual aspect is the relative starkness of the field. A man holding an equilateral cross is one of the few random elements included. It is possible that the bit of unfinished design to the left of the top medallion is the beginning of an inscription in Armenian.

Plate 35 is more like the rugs in Plates 30 and 31, with many different motifs filling in the available field, birds, goats, medallions. A pair of confronted falcons mark the center of the rug, and there is an equilateral cross just below the date. The letters following the date are incomplete.

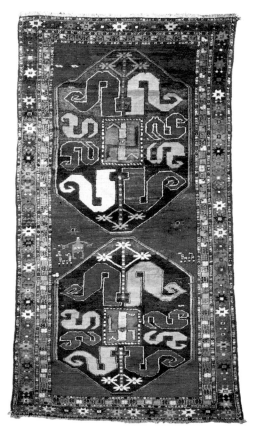

PLATE 35                          PLATE 36

## PLATE 35: KARABAGH *VISHAPAGORG*
### "CLOUDBAND DESIGN"   4'6" x 7'

Dated 1918 and Inscribed

COLORS:  Henna, dark blue, abrashed medium blue, dark brown, tan, ivory, pink, orange.

WARP:     WOOL, TAN AND NATURAL, 3 STRANDS, Z-SPIN, S-PLY

WEFT:      WOOL, FADED ORANGE, 2 STRANDS, Z-SPIN, S-PLY, 2 SHOOTS

PILE:       WOOL, 2 STRANDS, Z-SPIN, S-PLY

KNOT:     GHIORDES, 56/inch

EDGES:   FLAT, DARK RED           ENDS:   FRINGED ENDS

## PLATE 36: KARABAGH *VISHAPAGORG*
### "CLOUDBAND DESIGN"   4' x 7'6"

Uninscribed

COLORS:  Henna, dark blue, abrashed medium blue, gold, tan, ivory, coral, aniline purple, black.

WARP:     WOOL, NATURAL AND BROWN, 3 STRANDS, Z-SPIN, S-PLY

WEFT:      WOOL, TAN, 2 STRANDS, Z-SPIN, S-PLY, 2 SHOOTS

PILE:       WOOL, 2 STRANDS, Z-SPIN, S-PLY

KNOT:     GHIORDES, 81/inch

EDGES:   FLAT, DARK RED      ENDS:   FRINGED ENDS

## PLATE 37: **KARABAGH** "SAW-TOOTH MEDALLION"

4'5" x 7'8"

Dated 1838
INSCRIPTION: **11838** + **AMI**

This rug, and the six examples that follow, are representatives of a family of Karabagh weaving closely identified with Armenians. Many similar inscribed examples are known. In these rugs, the effect is of a dark blue field cut away in a saw-toothed pattern to reveal an underlying red field. (In one example below, Plate 37, the underlying field is blue and the medallions are red, an unusual though logical variation.) Blossoms strung along a vine outline each medallion just within the jagged edge, and a double cross (made up of the St. Andrew's Cross and the equilateral cross superimposed) forms the center of each medallion.

The colors of this simple rug have mellowed beautifully with time. Classic borders enclose a classic field, cut into a series of saw-toothed diamond-shaped medallions, stacked as on a pole. The rug is crowded with childish representations of animals and human figures, random medallions and false starts, meticulously shaped crosses. The awkwardness of the date implies that it was copied by an illiterate weaver.

PLATE 37

KARABAGH "SAW-TOOTH MEDALLION"   4'5" x 7'8"
Dated 1838

COLORS:   Maroon, henna, pink, medium blue, medium green, straw yellow, ochre,
dark brown, ivory, black.

WARP:     WOOL, NATURAL AND BROWN, 3 STRANDS, Z-SPIN, S-PLY

WEFT:     WOOL, TAN, 3 STRANDS, Z-SPIN, S-PLY, 2 SHOOTS

PILE:     WOOL, 2 STRANDS, Z-SPIN, S-PLY

KNOT:     GHIORDES, ca. 49/inch

EDGES:    FLAT, RED

ENDS:     UNRAVELLED

PREVIOUSLY PUBLISHED: Armenian Rugs — The Gregorian Collection (Michigan)

PLATE 38: **KARABAGH** "SAW-TOOTH MEDALLION"
3'9" x 13'5"   Dated April 14, 1858 and Inscribed
INSCRIPTION: (unclear)

PLATE 39: **KARABAGH** "SAW-TOOTH MEDALLION"
3'2" x 11'10"   Dated 1906 and Inscribed
INSCRIPTION: **1906 TIV SYOLOMAN A GRIGORIANTS**

The classic Karabagh in Plate 38 is less whimsical than most in the matter of secondary ornamentation. The color balance is superb. The particular rose-pink of the inner field is the Armenian insect red related to the cochineal of the New World. A legendary dye of historic Armenia, it often figured as a prize in tributory lists. Our word 'crimson' comes from its Arabic name, 'Qermez.'

Dated a half-century later, Plate 39 is similar in size, design, color and placement of the inscription. It is simpler and more open in its pattern, however, and a little finer in weave. A beautiful, but relatively common henna red has replaced the exotic insect-derived crimson. Note the many pairs of confronted birds and the ornate crosses scattered throughout the design.

PLATE 38

PLATE 39

## PLATE 38: KARABAGH "SAW-TOOTH MEDALLION"   3'9" x 13'5"
Dated April 14, 1858 and Inscribed

COLORS:  Rose, henna, dark brown, blue, ivory, gold, tan, pink, green, orange.

WARP:     WOOL, TAN, IVORY AND GREY, 2 STRANDS, Z-SPIN, S-PLY

WEFT:      WOOL, TAN, 2 STRANDS, Z-SPIN, S-PLY, 2 SHOOTS

PILE:       WOOL, 2 STRANDS, Z-SPIN, S-PLY

KNOT:      GHIORDES, ca. 56/inch

EDGES:    MISSING          ENDS:  UNRAVELLED

## PLATE 39: KARABAGH "SAW-TOOTH MEDALLION"   3'2" x 11'10"
Dated 1906 and Inscribed

COLORS:  Magenta, rose, henna, dark and medium blue, medium green, orange, ochre,
dark brown, ivory.

WARP:     WOOL, BROWN AND NATURAL, 3 STRANDS, Z-SPIN, S-PLY

WEFT:      WOOL, BROWN, 2 STRANDS, S-SPIN, Z-PLY, 2 SHOOTS

PILE:       WOOL, 2 STRANDS, S-SPIN, Z-PLY

KNOT:      GHIORDES, ca. 64/inch

EDGES:    FLAT, RED          ENDS:  KILIM FOLDED AND SEWN; UNRAVELLED

PREVIOUSLY PUBLISHED: (38) The Gregorian Collection Of Armenian Rugs
(Dartmouth), Weavers, Merchants, Kings (Fort Worth); (38,39) Armenian Rugs —
The Gregorian Collection (Michigan)

PLATE 40: **KARABAGH** "STEPPED MEDALLION"
3' x 10'7"   Dated 1897 and Inscribed
INSCRIPTION: **1897 AMI DZHAN.AVAFOV**

PLATE 41: **KARABAGH** "SAW-TOOTH MEDALLION"
4'4" x 9'   Dated Feb. 26, 1909 and Inscribed
INSCRIPTION: **MAGTAGH ADAMEANTZ 19 2/26 09 AMI**

Plate 40 shows a rug in which the outline of the traditional medallion has been softened from a bold saw-tooth to a gentle stepped outline. The cross in the center of each medallion has been reworked into a floral motif while the other stylistic elements remain unchanged. The rug is carefully composed and beautifully inscribed, as dignified and as impersonal as the weaver could create.

Plate 41 is an exceptionally handsome piece, with a deep pile of glossy wool and rich coloring. Magtagh is a sacrifice: it may be a name or it may imply that someone named Adamian was made a martyr on the date commemorated. The many crosses within the deep blue medallions seem to support this interpretation.

PLATE 40                                                            PLATE 41

# PLATE 40: KARABAGH "STEPPED MEDALLION"   3' x 10'7"
Dated 1897 and Inscribed

COLORS:  Henna, tan, ivory, light blue, dark blue, gold, yellow, coral.

WARP:     WOOL, NATURAL, 2 STRANDS, Z-SPIN, S-PLY

WEFT:     WOOL, HENNA, 3 STRANDS, Z-SPIN, S-PLY, 3 SHOOTS

PILE:     WOOL, 2 STRANDS, Z-SPIN, S-PLY

KNOT:     GHIORDES, 63/inch

EDGES:    FLAT, HENNA

ENDS:      KILIM PLAITED FOLDED AND SEWN; KILIM WITH FRINGE


# PLATE 41: KARABAGH "SAW-TOOTH MEDALLION"   4'4" x 9'
Dated Feb. 26, 1909 and Inscribed

COLORS:  Henna, dark brown, ivory, light blue, dark blue, yellow, orange.

WARP:     WOOL, NATURAL AND RED, 3 STRANDS, Z-SPIN, S-PLY

WEFT:     WOOL, BROWN AND RED, 3 STRANDS, Z-SPIN, S-PLY, 2 SHOOTS

PILE:     WOOL, 2 STRANDS, Z-SPIN, S-PLY

KNOT:     GHIORDES, 42/INCH

EDGES:    FLAT, HENNA      ENDS:     KILIM WITH PLAIT (BOTH)

## PLATE 42: **KARABAGH** "SAW-TOOTH MEDALLION"

4'3" x 7'7"

Ca. 1920, Inscribed
INSCRIPTION: **S.M.**

This rug was described by its seller as a wedding rug: in the upper field there is a female figure on the left and a male figure on the right, with two initials below the female figure. Both stand with arms akimbo, in the classic Caucasian mountaineer attitude of defiance. Rugs of this design family are usually 10' long or more; the rug in Plate 37 is the same size as this example, but was designed to be short, with three finished medallions. In this rug the third medallion has been left incomplete to accomodate the figures and the inscription. Although this is a relatively modern rug, the design and colors are completely traditional.

PLATE 42

KARABAGH "SAW-TOOTH MEDALLION"   4'3" x 7'7"
Ca. 1920, Inscribed

COLORS:  Magenta, coral, pink, yellow, dark, medium and light blue, medium green,
tan, ivory, chestnut, dark brown.

WARP:    WOOL, BROWN AND TAN, 3 STRANDS, Z-SPIN, S-PLY

WEFT:    WOOL, CHESTNUT, 2 STRANDS, Z-SPIN, S-PLY, 2 SHOOTS

PILE:    WOOL, 2 STRANDS, Z-SPIN, S-PLY

KNOT:    GHIORDES, ca. 48/inch

EDGES:   FLAT, CHESTNUT

ENDS:    KILIM FOLDED AND SEWN; KILIM

## PLATE 43: **KARABAGH** "SAW-TOOTH MEDALLION"

4'5" x 9'

Ca. 1900, Inscribed
INSCRIPTION: **SATENIK**

This rug is noteworthy for its reversal of the usual color scheme (red on blue, rather than vice-versa) and for its primitive charm. In addition to the name of the Armenian girl who wove this rug, the pattern includes many motifs we have come to recognize as typically Armenian: birds, especially falcons in confronted pairs; human and animal figures; ornate crosses. Notice how the bird motif is added even to the meandering vine pattern of the main border.

In the lower left a human figure and a medallion-enclosed cross are juxtaposed. Other motifs like dippers or chalices turned on their sides may be compared with the crucible (*krah*) depicted in Plate 68 below. The poor quality of the  wool in this rug, and the many changes of dye-lots, suggest that it was created under impoverished circumstances. Nevertheless, it stands as a testament to the imagination and artistic sense of its obscure weaver.

PLATE 43

## KARABAGH "SAW-TOOTH MEDALLION" 4'5" x 9'
Ca. 1900, Inscribed

COLORS:  Henna, orange, gold, yellow, dark blue, dark green, dark brown, ivory, natural tan, aniline purple.

WARP:    WOOL, BROWN AND NATURAL, 3 STRANDS, Z-SPIN, S-PLY

WEFT:    WOOL, YELLOW, RED AND TAN, 2 STRANDS, Z-SPIN, S-PLY, 2 SHOOTS

PILE:     WOOL, 2 STRANDS, Z-SPIN, S-PLY

KNOT:    GHIORDES, ca. 42/inch

EDGES:  FLAT, MULTI-COLOR

ENDS:    PLAITED; UNRAVELLED

PLATE 44: **KARABAGH** "MODIFIED SAW-TOOTH MEDALLION"

5'3" x 10'9"

Ca. 1900, Inscribed

INSCRIPTION: **MA** + (red)
**HA FA Y M AM ETS** (ivory)

This rug recalls the classic pattern shown in the preceding examples, but presents many individual variations. A rug of this size normally is woven over a period of several years: in this example there was probably another weaver after the first 18" had been completed. The design of the main border and its guard borders changes completely at this point. Near the top of the rug a few Armenian letters in red appear; the inscription seems as random as the reindeer, human figures, trees and chickens similarly scattered across the rug. On completion of the fourth medallion, however, space was left for a longer inscription. At the end of the field more letters are woven, this time in white. The design is totally interrupted by this addition. Note also the ornate crosses carefully worked into the second medallion. Despite the many irregularities, this rug achieves great harmony of color and design.

PLATE 44

KARABAGH "MODIFIED SAW-TOOTH MEDALLION"    5'3" x 10'9"
Ca. 1900, Inscribed

COLORS:  Dark brown, maroon, henna red, rose red, dark and light blue, dark and light
         green, coral, yellow, orange.

WARP:    WOOL, TAN WITH BROWN, 3 STRANDS, Z-SPIN, S-PLY

WEFT:     WOOL, NATURAL, 2 STRANDS, Z-SPIN, S-PLY, 2 SHOOTS

PILE:    WOOL, 2 STRANDS, Z-SPIN, S-PLY

KNOT:    GHIORDES, ca. 42/inch

EDGES:   FLAT, TAN

ENDS:    UNRAVELLED

## PLATE 45: **KARABAGH** "MODIFIED SAW-TOOTH MEDALLION"

3'3" x 14'

Dated 1901 and Inscribed

INSCRIPTION: **1901 TIV**
**T. TS. S.**
**GH. A. O.**

In this variation, the partial medallions on either side of the main central row are more fully realized than usual; furthermore, the medallions are not strung as on a pole, but drawn separately. The most extraordinary thing about this particular rug is that it was woven 'upside-down'; that is, the end with the inscription is, as is usual, the final part of the rug to be completed. This means that not only the inscription was woven from top to bottom, but also the little birds and other figures which are scattered about. Note that this rug is missing its outer guard border, presumably a narrow blue band with rosettes to match the inner guard.

PLATE 45

KARABAGH "MODIFIED SAW-TOOTH MEDALLION"   3'3" x 14'
Dated 1901 and Inscribed

COLORS: Magenta, henna, pink, dark and medium blue, gold, yellow, orange, ivory,
         dark brown.

WARP:    WOOL, NATURAL, 2 STRANDS, Z-SPIN, S-PLY

WEFT:    WOOL, BROWN, 2 STRANDS, Z-SPIN, S-PLY, 3 SHOOTS

PILE:     WOOL, 2 STRANDS, Z-SPIN, S-PLY

KNOT:    GHIORDES, ca. 42/inch

EDGES:   MISSING

ENDS:    UNRAVELLED

PLATE 46: **KARABAGH** "MODIFIED SAW-TOOTH MEDALLION"

4'8" x 6'8"

Dated 1917 and Inscribed
INSCRIPTION: **B A**
                **1917 TIV A B**

This is an exceptionally dainty, fine Karabagh. It could easily be mistaken for an Ahar or village Tabriz rug. The colors are classic to the southern Caucasus and to Azerbaijan province: gold, ivory, green, russet. By the simple artistic expedient of shrinking the jagged-edged medallions in relation to the size of the rug, a jewel-like expanse of plain field has been created. The weaver has shown uncharacteristic restraint in leaving the plain field empty.

PLATE 46

KARABAGH "MODIFIED SAW-TOOTH MEDALLION"   4'8" x 6'8"
Dated 1917 and Inscribed

COLORS:  Henna, russet, coral, gold, pink, light blue, green, dark brown, black, natural brown, ivory and grey.

WARP:    WOOL, BROWN AND NATURAL, 3 STRANDS, Z-SPIN, S-PLY

WEFT:    WOOL, GOLD, 3 STRANDS, Z-SPIN, S-PLY, 1 SHOOT

PILE:    WOOL, 2 STRANDS, Z-SPIN, S-PLY

KNOT:    GHIORDES, ca. 45/inch

EDGES:   FLAT, DARK BROWN

ENDS:    UNRAVELLED

PREVIOUSLY PUBLISHED: The Gregorian Collection Of Armenian Rugs (Dartmouth); Armenian Rugs — The Gregorian Collection (Michigan)

## PLATE 47: **KARABAGH** "TWO MEDALLION DESIGN"

5'7" x 7'7"

Dated 1919, 1927 and Inscribed
INSCRIPTION: **1991 TIV T.A.** (ivory)
                **1927 TIV** (blue)
                unclear initials (teal)

In this rug both color and design have been reduced to their simplest elements. The medallion is not stepped, saw-toothed or edged with finials; small dashes are the only ornament to its outline. A deep red, two blues and a gold supplement the natural dark brown and ivory of the wool. There are a few random elements, but much of the field is left bare. The ancient tree motif stands out starkly. This rug like that in Plate 16 was left incomplete in 1919 and finished much later, presumably by another hand.

PLATE 47

KARABAGH "TWO MEDALLION DESIGN"   5'7" x 7'7"
Dated 1919, 1927 and Inscribed

COLORS:  Wine red, dark blue, teal, natural dark brown, gold, ivory.

WARP:    WOOL, DARK AND LIGHT BROWN, 3 STRANDS, Z-SPIN, S-PLY

WEFT:    WOOL, DARK BROWN, Z-SPIN, S-PLY, 2 SHOOTS

PILE:    WOOL, 2 STRANDS, Z-SPIN, S-PLY

KNOT:    GHIORDES, ca. 42/inch

EDGES:   FLAT, RED

ENDS:    FRINGED

PLATE 48: **KARABAGH** "THREE MEDALLION DESIGN"

4'3" x 6'5"

Dated 1922 and Inscribed
INSCRIPTION: **1922 TIV/SOGHER**

This rug combines design elements characteristic of Shirvan and Karabagh. The
traditional medallion design is off-set by corners that enclose the European rose-motif.
Within the central medallion is a confronted pair of falcons and at the top, a small cross.
The bottom medallion shows attempts at representing a naturalistic bunch of grapes and
a rosebud as well as more primitive motifs. Among the many wild and charming figures
scattered throughout the field, notice the high-necked, high-tailed horse in the middle
right, with a partially completed human figure on its back.

PLATE 48

KARABAGH "THREE MEDALLION DESIGN"    4'3" x 6'5"
Dated 1922 and Inscribed

COLORS:   Dark brown, medium and dark blue, red, rose, orange, gold, yellow, green,
          ivory, aniline purple.

WARP:     WOOL, NATURAL, 3 STRANDS, Z-SPIN, S-PLY

WEFT:     WOOL, TAN AND BROWN, 3 STRANDS, Z-SPIN, S-PLY, 2 SHOOTS

PILE:     WOOL, 2 STRANDS, Z-SPIN, S-PLY

EDGES:    FLAT, BLUE AND YELLOW

ENDS:     KILIM FOLDED AND SEWN

## PLATE 49: **KARABAGH** *VISHAPAGORG* "EAGLE DESIGN"

4'8" x 8'

Dated 1927 and Inscribed
INSCRIPTION: **1927 TVARVART**

Once known as the 'eagle kazak', this design has been linked with the double-headed eagle motif as well as other ancient designs of the region. It is now classed by most experts as a pattern typical of Karabagh. Stylistically it bears a close resemblance to the so-called "Leshgi Star" design, e.g. Plates 91 and 92.

In Armenia the "eagle design" is considered to be another family of *Vishapagorg*. The existence of numerous inscribed examples implies that this, like the 'cloudband' and 'saw-tooth medallion' rugs shown above, is a typically Armenian form of Karabagh weaving.

A late example, this rug is woven with great exactness: the small motifs in the field, often personal and randomly placed, are here treated in a strict and symmetrical manner. A high proportion of the dyes show fading, suggesting poor quality. Nevertheless, the design is a classic one beautifully executed, and the letters of the inscription are drawn with an artistic flourish.

PLATE 49

KARABAGH *VISHAPAGORG* "EAGLE DESIGN"    4'8" x 8'
Dated 1927 and Inscribed

COLORS:  Red, dark brown, ivory, dark blue, purple, pink, orange, gold, yellow.

WARP:     WOOL, NATURAL, TAN, BROWN, 3 STRANDS, Z-SPIN, S-PLY

WEFT:     WOOL, NATURAL, TAN, 2 STRANDS, Z-SPIN, S-PLY, 2 SHOOTS

PILE:     WOOL, 2 STRANDS, Z-SPIN, S-PLY

KNOT:     GHIORDES, 49/inch

EDGES:    FLAT, ORANGE

ENDS:     PLAITED; KILIM WITH FRINGE

## PLATE 50: **KARABAGH** "OPEN FIELD DESIGN"

4'10" x 8'7"

Dated 1927 and Inscribed
INSCRIPTION: **1927 TIV, GIG OLGHA TSARIANTS GEGEL**

This rug has suffered extensive damage and patching. Apparently the weaver intended a small inscription in the field, for a few letters in blue do appear in the lower left corner. The final inscription, however, is placed traditionally in a plain area left between the end of the field and the border. The ornate style of the border is in contrast to the simplicity of the field: the leaf motifs are woven in a shape reminiscent of the ancient *Vishap*. The Armenian rug from Feridun shown in Plate 102 shows similar drawing.

PLATE 50

KARABAGH "OPEN FIELD DESIGN"   4'10" x 8'7"
Dated 1927 and Inscribed

COLORS:   Henna, dark and light blue, gold, light green, dark and light brown, ivory,
          tan, pink.

WARP:     WOOL, IVORY, 4 STRANDS, Z-SPIN, S-PLY

WEFT:     WOOL, TAN, 2 STRANDS, Z-SPIN, S-PLY, 2 SHOOTS

PILE:     WOOL, 2 STRANDS, Z-SPIN, S-PLY

KNOT:     GHIORDES, ca. 56/inch

EDGES:    FLAT, TAN

ENDS:     KILIM FOLDED AND SEWN; UNRAVELLED

PLATE 51: **KARABAGH** "COVERED FIELD DESIGN"
3'11" x 12'3"   Dated 1904 and Inscribed
INSCRIPTION: **1904** (unclear) **AMI KHTSRI V.O.**

PLATE 52: **KARABAGH** "NOUSH DESIGN"
4'5" x 9'2"   Dated 1914 and Inscribed
INSCRIPTION: **1914 TIV VASIL+MOUTOCHO** (V)

In Plate 51, two borders of meandering vine enclose a field covered with columns of stylized blossoms. The pattern is as restrained as the coloration is flamboyant. A touch of whimsy on the part of the weaver has created a column of birds, animals and human figures along the right side of the field, but this touch only lasts for three-quarters of the rug's length.

Plate 52 is an essentially simple rug, the repeated motifs carefully alternated by row. A secondary diagonal pattern has been created by the colors used. Once again the cross in the inscription indicates a death.

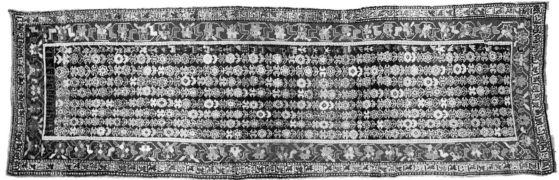

PLATE 51

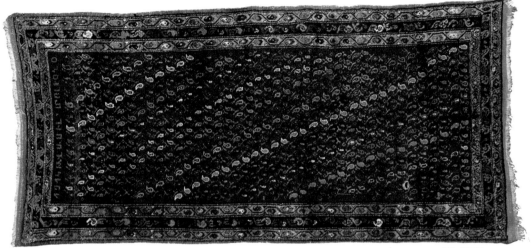

PLATE 52

## PLATE 51: KARABAGH "COVERED FIELD DESIGN"   3'11" x 12'3"
Dated 1904 and Inscribed

COLORS:   Magenta, scarlet, hot pink, orange, yellow, light green, dark brown, black,
aniline purple and pink.

WARP:   WOOL, BROWN AND WHITE, 3 STRANDS, Z-SPIN, S-PLY

WEFT:   WOOL, BROWN, 2 STRANDS, Z-SPIN, S-PLY, 2 SHOOTS

PILE:   WOOL, 2 STRANDS, Z-SPIN, S-PLY

KNOT:   GHIORDES, ca. 35/inch

EDGES:   FLAT, TAN   ENDS: KILIM FOLDED AND SEWN; UNRAVELLED

## PLATE 52: KARABAGH "NOUSH DESIGN"   4'5" x 9'2"
Dated 1914 and Inscribed

COLORS:   Maroon, henna, pink, light blue, gold, orange, chestnut and dark brown.

WARP:   WOOL, IVORY*

WEFT:   WOOL*

PILE:   WOOL*

KNOT:   GHIORDES,*

EDGES:   FLAT, CHESTNUT BROWN   ENDS:   KILIM UNRAVELLED

* Unavailable for technical analysis
PREVIOUSLY PUBLISHED: (51 and 52) The Gregorian Collection Of Armenian Rugs
(Dartmouth); (51) Armenian Rugs — The Gregorian Collection (Michigan)

PLATE 53: **KARABAGH** "NOUSH DESIGN"

4'5" x 8'2"

Dated Mar. 13, 1906 and Inscribed
INSCRIPTION: **19 3/13 06**

This austerely beautiful rug was woven as a commemorative. The birds in the border as
well as the somber colors suggest a funereal context, since in Armenian belief the
departed soul is represented by a bird. When the inscription appears in the center of a
rug, as in this case, it is clear that the weaving of the rug was dedicated to a memorial
purpose. This is a much greater committment of time, effort and emotion than the simple
inscribing of a rug already near completion. This impressive rug is a masterpiece of
understatement and rich, deep color.

PLATE 53

# KARABAGH "NOUSH DESIGN" 4'5" x 8'2"
Dated Mar. 13, 1906 and Inscribed

COLORS: Dark and light blue, medium green, red, yellow, ivory, brown.

WARP: WOOL, TAN AND BROWN TWISTED TOGETHER, 3 STRANDS, Z-SPIN, S-PLY

WEFT: WOOL, BROWN, 2 STRANDS, Z-SPIN, S-PLY, 2-3 SHOOTS

PILE: WOOL, 2 STRANDS, Z-SPIN, S-PLY

KNOT: GHIORDES, ca. 90/inch

EDGES: FLAT, ROSE RED

ENDS: UNRAVELLED

PREVIOUSLY PUBLISHED: The Gregorian Collection Of Armenian Rugs (Dartmouth); Weavers, Merchants, Kings (Fort Worth)

## PLATE 54: **KARABAGH** "COVERED FIELD DESIGN"

4'2" x 6'10"

Ca. 1890, Inscribed
### INSCRIPTION: **MIKHAEL SARKISIANTS**

This rug seems to be related to those in Plates 59-61 by proportion, simple repetitive design and use of color. This example is almost Asiatic in character, and is notable for being signed with the name of a male weaver. The pattern seems like a Caucasian interpretation of the Yomut Turkoman, with Caucasian borders, weave and coloring. The decision to inscribe the rug was made in the midst of creating another row of design. The ommission of a date is unusual.

PLATE 54

KARABAGH "COVERED FIELD DESIGN"   4'2" x 6'10"
Ca. 1890, Inscribed

COLORS:  Henna, rose, medium blue, light green, ivory, tan, black.

WARP:     WOOL, FADED ORANGE AND TAN, 2 STRANDS, Z-SPIN, S-PLY

WEFT:     WOOL, ORANGE AND RED, 2 STRANDS, Z-SPIN, S-PLY, 2 SHOOTS

PILE:      WOOL, 2 STRANDS, Z-SPIN, S-PLY

KNOT:     GHIORDES, ca. 49/inch

EDGES:    FLAT, ROSE RED

ENDS:     UNRAVELLED

PREVIOUSLY PUBLISHED: The Gregorian Collection Of Armenian Rugs (Dartmouth)

## PLATE 55: **KARABAGH** "COVERED FIELD DESIGN"

3'7" x 8'2"

Dated 1916 and Inscribed
INSCRIPTION **1916 TIV** (garbled letters)

A simple, stylized rug using an overall pattern of blossoms with geometric stems and leaves. Each is enclosed in a diamond and the diamonds are linked by small equilateral crosses. Wool and colors are excellent. This type of design, with narrow borders and a straight-forward unadorned pattern is woven throughout the Caucasus and is not specifically Armenian. It is a classic pattern for many weavers of different ethnic groups.

PLATE 55

KARABAGH "COVERED FIELD"   3'7" x 8'2"
Dated 1916 and Inscribed

COLORS:  Henna, dark brown, ivory, dark blue, dark green, yellow, pink, orange.

WARP:    WOOL, NATURAL AND BROWN, 3 STRANDS, Z-SPIN, S-PLY

WEFT:    WOOL, TAN, 2 STRANDS, Z-SPIN, S-PLY, 2 SHOOTS

PILE:    WOOL, 2 STRANDS, Z-SPIN, S-PLY

KNOT:    GHIORDES, 66/inch

EDGES:   FLAT, BROWN

ENDS:    KILIM FOLDED AND SEWN; KILIM WITH FRINGE

PLATE 56: **KARABAGH** "COVERED FIELD DESIGN"

4' x 8'6"

Dated 1929 and Inscribed
INSCRIPTION: **1929 TIV KHAGIGANILOV** (UNCLEAR)

This piece is more complex than the preceding example, suggesting architectural ornament. It can be compared with the 19th century Gendje in Plate 27. The rich overall
pattern is like a mosaic tile, and the mood is sustained by narrow, small-figured borders.

It has been suggested that Armenian rugs inscribed like this example, in an extra apron
of color lying outside the design of the rug, were woven this way for a special purpose.
The owner could cut off the inscription should an Armenian identity ever prove to be a
political liability, without harming the rug.

PLATE 56

KARABAGH "COVERED FIELD"   4' x 8'6"
Dated 1929 and Inscribed

COLORS:  Henna, dark brown, light blue, dark blue, ivory, gold, yellow.

WARP:     WOOL, TAN, NATURAL AND BROWN, 3 STRANDS, Z-SPIN, S-PLY

WEFT:     WOOL, DARK BROWN AND TAN, 2 STRANDS, Z-SPIN, S-PLY,
          2 SHOOTS

PILE:     WOOL, 2 STRANDS, Z-SPIN, S-PLY

KNOT:     GHIORDES, 48/inch

EDGES:    FLAT TAN

ENDS:     KILIM WITH PLAIT AND FRINGE; KILIM WITH FRINGE

## PLATE 57: **KARABAGH** "NOUSH DESIGN"

4'9" x 8'6"

Dated June 26, 1810
INSCRIPTION: **1810 AMI HOINSI 26**

The outermost border of this old rug is a rosette motif most often found on "eagle design" *Vishapagorg* rugs from Karabagh. The main border design is found on many Caucasian pieces both Kazak and Karabagh, and the inner guard border bears a stylized version of the European rose motif.

This eclectic collection of borders encloses a very simple and traditional large-scale "paisley" pattern. In scale it is similar to that of the 1881 Gendje in Plate 26. Rosettes and birds fill in the available space around the main design, and the exact date is clearly inscribed across the top.

PLATE 57

KARABAGH "NOUSH DESIGN"   4'9" x 8'6"
Dated June 26, 1810

COLORS:  Henna, abrashed red, dark brown, red-brown, tan, abrashed green, indigo, ivory, yellow, faded purple.

WARP:    WOOL, BROWN AND TAN, 3 STRANDS, Z-SPIN, S-PLY

WEFT:    WOOL, TAN, 2 STRANDS, Z-SPIN, S-PLY, 2 SHOOTS

PILE:    WOOL, 2 STRANDS, S-SPIN, Z-PLY

KNOT:    GHIORDES, 48/inch

EDGES:   FLAT, GOLD

ENDS:    SELF BRAID, UNRAVELLED

PLATE 58: **KARABAGH**

4'2" x 6'3"   Dated 1899 and Inscribed

INSCRIPTION: **M.G. 1899 TIV**


PLATE 59: **KARABAGH**

4'5" x 6'8"   Dated 1899 and Inscribed

INSCRIPTION: **SIGOGHALOS VARTANIANTS 1899 AMI**

These two rugs, and the two shown in Plates 60 and 61, are part of a group of inscribed Armenian rugs that measure approximately 4 x 7 and effectively contrast warm red fields with rich green borders. They all seem to have been woven between 1890 and 1915, presumably in the same village or group of villages. Plate 58 uses a whimsically stylized bird motif in an over-all pattern. Well-drawn crosses and primitive falcons are scattered throughout the field.

The significance of Plate 59 is obscure. Vases of roses are depicted, each of which holds a cross in addition to the blossoms. The inscription, a man's name and the date, is shown in the shape of a salt-bag. Flat-woven salt-bags are a common part of the Mid-Eastern shepherd's equipment; the precious mineral is carried in a sack which has a tube-like opening just big enough for him to insert his hand and bring out a small measure. Considering the many crosses, it is quite likely that the reference here is to the salt of baptism, and the rug commemorates a sacrament.

PLATE 58                              PLATE 59

## PLATE 58: KARABAGH    4'2" x 6'3"
Dated 1899 and Inscribed

| | |
|---|---|
| COLORS: | Magenta, henna, gold, pink, dark green, medium blue, ivory, dark brown, natural tan. |
| WARP: | WOOL, NATURAL, 2 STRANDS, Z-SPIN, S-PLY |
| WEFT: | WOOL, HENNA, 2 STRANDS, Z-SPIN, S-PLY, 2 SHOOTS |
| PILE: | WOOL, 2 STRANDS, Z-SPIN, S-PLY |
| KNOT: | GHIORDES, ca. 72/inch |
| EDGES: | FLAT, DARK RED |
| ENDS: | KILIM |

## PLATE 59: KARABAGH    4'5" x 6'8"
Dated 1899 and Inscribed

| | |
|---|---|
| COLORS: | Henna, wine red, dark blue, light blue, dark green, light green, brown, black, orange, pink, purple. |
| WARP: | WOOL, IVORY AND BROWN, 2 STRANDS, Z-SPIN, S-PLY |
| WEFT: | WOOL, HENNA, 2 STRANDS, Z-SPIN, S-PLY, 2 SHOOTS |
| PILE: | WOOL 2 STRANDS, Z-SPIN, S-PLY |
| KNOT: | GHIORDES 56/inch |
| EDGES: | FLAT HENNA |
| ENDS: | FRAYED; BOUND WITH CLOTH |

PLATE 60: **KARABAGH**
3'6" x 7'6"   Dated 1915 and Inscribed
INSCRIPTION: **1915 TIV** (unclear) **SATEGH AF DZVOVI**

PLATE 61: **KARABAGH**
4'1" x 6'6"   Dated 1909 and Inscribed
INSCRIPTION: **SATENIG AROUSHANIANTS 1909 TIV**

Plate 60 is another fine example of the ability of Armenian weavers in Karabagh to use
large numbers of bright colors with taste and skill. The deep green of the border balances
the clear red of the field, and the wonderfully eccentric collection of motifs is crisply
delineated. The pattern is a form of the Fereghan design, interpreted in a highly
individualistic manner. In the rug's center there are pairs of birds confronted in classic
Armenian fashion.

Plate 61 employs almost the same design, but woven on a larger scale, more stylized
and less personal than the other. The finials of the large central motifs may be a late
interpretation of the bird-headed finials seen in earlier rugs (cf. Plate 69 below). Color
run has dyed the ivory borders pink; the inscription is clearly the work of a literate
weaver.

PLATE 61

PLATE 60

## PLATE 60: KARABAGH   3'6" x 7'6"
Dated 1915 and Inscribed

COLORS:  Magenta, henna, orange, pink, dark and light green, dark and medium blue, ivory, dark brown.

WARP:    WOOL, FADED RED, 3 STRANDS, Z-SPIN, S-PLY

WEFT:    WOOL, RUST, 2 STRANDS, Z-SPIN, S-PLY, 1 SHOOT

PILE:    WOOL, 2-STRANDS, S-SPIN, Z-PLY

KNOT:    GHIORDES, ca. 63/inch

EDGES:   FLAT, RED          ENDS:  UNRAVELLLED

## PLATE 61: KARABAGH   4'1" x 6'6"
Dated 1909 and Inscribed

COLORS:  Magenta, henna, gold, yellow, pink, dark blue, dark green, dark brown, ivory.

WARP:    WOOL, NATURAL, 3 STRANDS, Z-SPIN, S-PLY

WEFT:    WOOL, TAN, 2 STRANDS, Z-SPIN, S-PLY, 2 SHOOTS

PILE:    WOOL, 2 STRANDS, Z-SPIN, S-PLY

KNOT:    GHIORDES, ca. 72/inch

EDGES:   FLAT, DARK RED        ENDS:  KILIM FOLDED AND SEWN

PREVIOUSLY PUBLISHED: (60) The Gregorian Collection Of Armenian Rugs (Dartmouth); Armenian Rugs — The Gregorian Collection (Michigan)

## PLATE 62: **KARABAGH**

4′6″ x 8′10″

Dated March 11, 1917 and Inscribed

INSCRIPTION: **1917 TIV MARDI 11** (Top)
                             **NAS** (Top Right)
                             **NA** (Lower Left)
                             **N** (Bottom Left)

This rug resembles the red and green Karabaghs shown in Plates 58-62, but it is longer and not so intense in color. A repeated vase design is used, and the sides of the vases are drawn in a manner reminiscent of the bird/fish motif in Plate 58. The vases themselves are arranged in diagonal stripes of light and dark, and the main border design is the European rose motif.

The chief points of interest in this rug are the small figures in the field, Armenian letters, birds on branches, a cross, a goat, a man with one arm raised. Their childish simplicity is an effective contrast with the harmonious repetitive pattern.

PLATE 62

**KARABAGH**   4'6" x 8'10"
Dated March 11, 1917 and Inscribed

COLORS:  Henna, dark blue, light blue, gold, yellow, medium green, dark brown, ivory,
purple, pink.

WARP:  WOOL, NATURAL AND TAN 3 STRANDS, Z-SPIN, S-PLY

WEFT:  WOOL, NATURAL AND TAN 3 STRANDS, Z-SPIN, S-PLY, 2 SHOOTS

PILE:  WOOL, 2 STRANDS, Z-SPIN, S-PLY

KNOT:  GHIORDES, 48/inch

EDGES:  FLAT, BROWN

ENDS:  FRINGED; KILIM WITH FRINGE

PLATE 63: **KARABAGH** "SHEMAKHA DESIGN"
4' x 9'4"   Dated March 1899 and Inscribed
INSCRIPTION: **I 1899 MARDI ATSOUGH**

PLATE 64: **KARABAGH** "SHEMAKHA DESIGN"
4'7" x 8'10"   Dated 1928 and Inscribed
INSCRIPTION: **1928 TIV DZNT. A.**

The graceful medallions in these rugs recall the type of *Vishapagorg* known as 'eagle' (Plate 49). Designs of this type are common to parts of Armenia and Georgia. It is most often seen in the embroidered flat-weaves of Shemakha (Sumakh) near Gendje. There is a striking similarity between these rugs despite the difference in age: it is noteworthy that the earlier rug has less spontaneity than the newer example.

Plate 64 has strongly Anatolian colors. The effect is enhanced by the unfortunate practice of severe bleaching still common treatment for old rugs found in Turkey, as this was. Although this is a late rug it has the whimsy of an earlier creation. On either side of the third medallion stand a pair of soldiers, dressed in flared breeches and double-breasted coats. The inscription may be short for dznount, 'birth'.

PLATE 63                                                    PLATE 64

## PLATE 63: KARABAGH "SHEMAKHA DESIGN"   4' x 9'4"
Dated 1899 and Inscribed

COLORS:   Magenta, henna, coral, orange, dark brown, medium and light green, ivory, aniline purple.

WARP:     WOOL, BROWN AND NATURAL, 3 Z-SPIN, S-PLY

WEFT:     WOOL, RED AND WHITE, 2 STRANDS, Z-SPIN, S-PLY, 1 SHOOT

PILE:     WOOL, 2 STRANDS, S-SPIN, Z-PLY

KNOT:     GHIORDES, ca. 90/inch

EDGES:    FLAT, CORAL              ENDS:    UNRAVELLED

## PLATE 64: KARABAGH "SHEMAKHA DESIGN"   4'7" x 8'10"
Dated 1928 and Inscribed

COLORS:   Dark and medium brown, dark and light rose, gold, green, ivory, aniline blue and light green (rug bleached).

WARP:     WOOL, BROWN AND NATURAL, 3 STRANDS, Z-SPIN, S-PLY

WEFT:     WOOL, BROWN, BLUE, AND TAN, 2 STRANDS, Z-SPIN, S-PLY, 2 SHOOTS

PILE:     WOOL, 2 STRANDS, S-SPIN, Z-PLY

KNOT:     GHIORDES, ca. 36/inch

EDGES:    FLAT, DARK BROWN        ENDS:    PLAIT

## PLATE 65: **KARABAGH** "LEMPE DESIGN"

3'9" x 9'

Dated 1831 (?) and Inscribed
INSCRIPTION: **P.I. M.K. 183 (1?) AMI**

This is a rug woven on a wool warp mixed with cotton, and wefted with cotton as well. Remarkably the cotton has not become fragile or ripped despite the heavy wear the rug has received. It is a wonderful example of ancient and modern motifs living comfortably together. A modified European rose pattern has been used for the border design, while the main field is notable for the large primitive peacocks that are so often associated with this design.

The use of cotton for warp and/or weft is a feature of many early "Lempe" rugs. It is not known where (or whether) the village of Lempe is, but the name is given to those Karabaghs of long proportion which feature eight-sided medallions of differing design, often accented by pairs of large confronted birds. The Soviet writer Kerimov places "Lempe" rugs in the region of Shusha in Karabagh.

PLATE 65

KARABAGH "LEMPE DESIGN"    3'9" x 9'
Dated 1831 (?) and Inscribed

COLORS:  Magenta, henna, dark and light blue, green, coral, yellow, dark brown, ivory.

WARP:    WOOL AND COTTON, WHITE AND FADED CORAL, 3 STRANDS,
         Z-SPIN, S-PLY

WEFT:    COTTON, WHITE, 2 STRANDS, 3 SHOOTS

PILE:    WOOL, 2 STRANDS, S-SPIN, Z-PLY

KNOT:    GHIORDES, ca. 64/inch

EDGES:   MISSING

ENDS:    KILIM UNRAVELLED

PLATE 66: **KARABAGH** "LEMPE DESIGN"

3'8" x 13'9"   Dated April 6, 1888 and Inscribed

INSCRIPTION: **TIATAEN SAFARIANTSO 1888 A 6 IL +
M.SI + SIMPA**

PLATE 67: **KARABAGH** "LEMPE DESIGN"

4'5" x 15'6"   Dated 1894 and Inscribed

INSCRIPTION: **1894 AMI** (unclear)

Each of these rugs, like the preceding earlier example, uses cotton as weft material. These two rugs bear many obvious similarities to each other, the most noticeable difference being that the peacocks of the 1888 rug have been replaced by small round medallions in the 1894 example.

In each rug, the large red medallions use a design similar to the "turtle" of Azerbaijani weaving. The color balance and design are so alike it is hard to believe that these are not both from the same village, possibly even the same family. The exact date and cross in the 1888 inscription indicate the commemoration of a death.

PLATE 66

PLATE 67

### PLATE 66: KARABAGH "LEMPE DESIGN"   3'8" x 13'9"
Dated April 6, 1888 and Inscribed

COLORS:  Dark blue, light blue, gold, dark gold, dark brown, ivory, coral, dark rose.

WARP:    WOOL, TAN AND BROWN, 3 STRANDS, Z-SPIN, S-PLY

WEFT:    COTTON, WHITE, 2 STRANDS, 4 SHOOTS

PILE:    WOOL, 2 STRANDS, Z-SPIN, S-PLY

KNOT:    GHIORDES, 80/inch

EDGES:   FLAT, DARK ROSE      ENDS:  KILIM FRINGED (BOTH)

### PLATE 67: KARABAGH "LEMPE DESIGN"   4'5" x 15'6"
Dated 1894 and Inscribed

COLORS:  Dark red, dark blue, light blue, gold, yellow, abrashed green, tan, ivory, black, coral.

WARP:    WOOL, TAN AND NATURAL, 3 STRANDS, Z SPIN, S-PLY

WEFT:    WOOL AND COTTON, WHITE AND BROWN, 3 STRANDS, Z-SPIN, S-PLY 2-3 SHOOTS

PILE:    WOOL, 2 STRANDS, Z-SPIN, S-PLY

KNOT:    GHIORDES, 81/inch

EDGES:   FLAT, HENNA      ENDS:   KILIM FOLDED AND SEWN; SHORT FRINGE

## PLATE 68: **KARABAGH** "LEMPE DESIGN"

3'11" x 9'

Ca. 1880, Inscribed
### INSCRIPTION: **KRAH**

This rug and the one following present apparent variations on the "Lempe" design. They are more complex than the preceding three examples, however, and do not use cotton in the foundation. In both of these rugs, Plates 68 and 69, the dark field is covered with small motifs.

The cryptic Armenian word *krah* (melting pot, crucible) appears near the center of this otherwise uninscribed rug. The small figures outlined in white next to the inscription may be taken as the crude representation of a ladle. We will never know why the weaver of this rug decided on such an inconspicuous and unlikely addition to her creation. In this rug, as in the preceding examples, traces of the "turtle" design can be seen in the main, red medallion.

PLATE 68

KARABAGH "LEMPE DESIGN"   3'11"x 9'
Ca. 1880, Inscribed

COLORS:  Magenta, henna, orange, yellow, pink, dark and medium blue, dark brown,
ivory, aniline purple.

WARP:     WOOL, NATURAL, 3 STRANDS, Z-SPIN, S-PLY

WEFT:     WOOL, RED, 2 STRANDS, Z-SPIN, S-PLY, 4 SHOOTS

PILE:     WOOL, 2 STRANDS, S-SPIN, Z-PLY

KNOT:     GHIORDES, ca. 77/inch

EDGES:    FLAT, HENNA

ENDS:     KILIM FOLDED AND SEWN; KILIM WITH FRINGE

PREVIOUSLY PUBLISHED: The Gregorian Collection Of Armenian Rugs (Dartmouth)

## PLATE 69: **KARABAGH** "LEMPE DESIGN"

4' x 15'

Dated 1904 and Inscribed
INSCRIPTION: **1904 IN MEMORY OF --** (unclear)

Another "Lempe design" with a covered rather than an open field. Potted plants and small medallions fill all the available space. The birds of the classic form of the design (Plate 65) are present here in memory, as bird-headed finials on the ivory main medallions. The strong contrasting colors give this old design a new and vivid interpretation.

It has been mentioned above, in the discussion of Plates 32 and 33, that confronted birds separated by a tree motif is an ancient design, traditional among Armenians, but also classic in Mesopotamian as well as later Persian and Indian art. One of the earliest forms is of two falcon-headed gods standing on either side of a tree. A small square bag hangs from each god's hand, and they are shown fertilizing the sacred tree with a pine cone dipped in pollen. This design was widely disseminated in rock-carvings.

In the rug under discussion a small square bag of similar design hangs from each bird's beak, and in the medallion that separates them a flattened tree is outlined in green. It can be a coincidence of pattern, or a survival.

PLATE 69

## KARABAGH "LEMPE DESIGN"  4' x 15'
Dated 1904 and Inscribed

COLORS:   Red, dark and light blue, dark brown, green, teal, pink, ivory,
                 natural tan, black.

WARP:      WOOL, BROWN AND IVORY, 2 STRANDS, Z-SPIN, S-PLY

WEFT:       WOOL, BROWN, 2 STRANDS, Z-SPIN, S-PLY, 2 SHOOTS

PILE:        WOOL, 2 STRANDS, Z-SPIN, S-PLY

KNOT:      GHIORDES, ca. 49/inch

EDGES:    FLAT, BROWN

ENDS:      KILIM FOLDED AND SEWN

PREVIOUSLY PUBLISHED: Weavers, Merchants and Kings (Fort Worth)

## PLATE 70: **KARABAGH *VISHAPAGORG*** "ARCHAIC DESIGN"

4'9" x 10'

Dated 1902
INSCRIPTION: **1902 AMI**

This is a relatively modern rug, yet it displays archaic design elements. This narrow-bordered palmette-patterned rug would not look out of place in the background of a Renaissance painting. As with so many of those early rugs, the border looks like a frame placed over and isolating a small piece of a much broader pattern. Typically Armenian are the crosses, birds, animal and human figures. The date and signature have been woven in twice, the second inscription being a mirror image of the first.

The major motifs in this rug are close relatives to those found in the classic "dragon-rugs" of 500 years ago. The *Vishap* are shown in rigid, geometric shapes forming the sides of each small central medallion. The design looks as though it may have been copied from a flat-woven or embroidered textile, possibly of much earlier vintage.

PLATE 70

KARABAGH *VISHAPAGORG* "ARCHAIC DESIGN"    4'9" x 10'
Dated 1902

COLORS:  Henna, dark blue, green, orange, yellow, light brown, ivory, bright red.

WARP:    WOOL, BROWN AND IVORY, 2 STRANDS, Z-SPIN, S-PLY

WEFT:    WOOL, TAN, 2 STRANDS, Z-SPIN, S-PLY, 2 SHOOTS

PILE:    WOOL, 2 STRANDS, Z-SPIN, S-PLY

KNOT:    GHIORDES, ca. 48/inch

EDGES:   NOT ORIGINAL

ENDS:    UNRAVELLED

PREVIOUSLY PUBLISHED: The Gregorian Collection Of Armenian Rugs (Dartmouth);
Weavers, Merchants and Kings (Fort Worth)

## PLATE 71: **SHUSHA KARABAGH**

4'9" x 7'11"

Dated 1900 and Inscribed
INSCRIPTION: **1900 TIV**
**S GH KH A DEGHYIA ROOSNA**
**PEGHLAROV**

This festive rug is typical of the heavy, thick-piled rugs woven near Shusha, in the southern Karabagh region. The inscription is hard to read, but seems to refer to new beginnings, an appropriate wish for 1900. This sense of celebration is emphasized by the dancing man clearly depicted in the upper right hand corner; he holds a flowing handkerchief in one hand and has the other on his hip. Also represented are small rugs, each with its own over-sized medallion, and a pair of horses with arched necks and tails. Rows of falcons support the inscription.

PLATE 71

## SHUSHA KARABAGH  4'9" x 7'11"
Dated 1900 and Inscribed

COLORS:  Red, coral, dark, medium and light blue, gold, yellow, green, dark brown, ivory, aniline purple, blue, pink

WARP:  WOOL, BROWN AND IVORY, 3 STRANDS, Z-SPIN, S-PLY

WEFT:  WOOL, TAN, 2 STRANDS, Z-SPIN, S-PLY, 3 SHOOTS

PILE:  2 STRANDS, S-SPIN, Z-PLY

KNOT:  GHIORDES, ca. 36/inch

EDGES:  FLAT, LIGHT BLUE

ENDS:  KILIM WITH PLAIT; KILIM FRINGED

PREVIOUSLY PUBLISHED: Armenian Rugs — The Gregorian Collection (Michigan)

## PLATE 72: **KARABAGH** "MODIFIED SALOR DESIGN"

4' x 7'10"

Dated 1922 and Inscribed
INSCRIPTION: **1922** (letters unclear)

This rug is similar in weave and basic design to Plate 71, but uses a motif less common to the Caucasus. The medallions are an enlarged adaptation of the gul of the Salor Turkomans. This combination of pattern and color invites comparison with the rugs of Chinese Turkestan. Within the context of this collection it is interesting to compare Plate 104, the inscribed Armenian rug from Turkestan. In both examples the same combination of Turkoman motifs has been used, but in the example from the Caucasus the weave has remained heavy and coarsely-knotted.

What ivory there once was in this rug has now been stained by the unstable reds and oranges so well-known in Caucasian rugs; furthermore, the only contrasting color, blue, was an aniline which has faded almost to grey. The happy result of these color changes is a glowing orange rug of great power and beauty.

PLATE 72

KARABAGH "MODIFIED SALOR DESIGN"    4' x 7'10"
Dated 1922 and Inscribed

COLORS:  Red, orange, coral, rose, dark brown, ivory, aniline blue.

WARP:     WOOL, IVORY AND TAN, 3 STRANDS, Z-SPIN, S-PLY

WEFT:     WOOL, BROWN, 2 STRANDS, Z-SPIN, S-PLY, 2 SHOOTS

PILE:      WOOL, 2 STRANDS, S-SPIN, Z-PLY

KNOT:     GHIORDES, ca. 48/inch

EDGES:    ROUND, MULTI-COLOR

ENDS:     SELF-BRAID WITH FRINGE

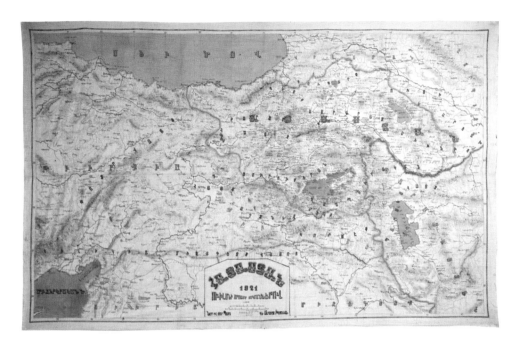

## THE REPUBLIC OF ARMENIA 1921

Armenia formed a Republic in 1918, uniting portions of Western
Armenia (ancient Armenia Minor) and Eastern Armenia (ancient
Armenia Major) as shown on this map. By the end of 1921 the
western portion had been relinquished and all that remained was
the eastern section around Lake Sevan. This forms the nucleus
of today's Soviet Socialist Republic. The twin symbols of modern
Armenia are the grape-vine and the rose.

# IV: PICTORIAL AND ROSE-PATTERNED KARABAGHS

During the 19th century Russian influence increased in the Transcaucasus, and many Armenians in the region began to look to the Tsar as a potential defender, a Christian patron against the Muslim world. Some Armenian intellectuals went to study in Russia, others to France, and signs of European influence began to show in carpet design as well as in political thought.

Since earliest times, Armenians had considered the rose to be a symbol of Armenia. Along with the bunch of grapes and the falcon/eagle it was seen in many stylized forms, carved on ancient churches, painted in illuminated manuscripts, embossed on metalwork, embroidered on Ecclesiastical garments. The popular male name Vartan — the name of the great hero who turned back the Persian conquest in 451 AD — means 'rose'. Thus it is not surprising that the realistic European-style rose captured the imagination of Armenian weavers and inspired a tradition that has lasted to present times.

The urge to emulate European arts caused another type of rug to come into being — hand-knotted copies of European tapestries and machine-loomed sentimental pictures. Typically, the weaver would present the exotic European picture horizontally. She, however, would be working vertically. Sometimes the urge to put in personal touches could not be suppressed, as in the Plate 82, where Armenian folk motifs fill the vertical space making an unlikely background for the horizontal picture. The Soviet rug (Plate 86) that completes this section has a bizarre charm which is the result of a curious juxtaposition. Pairs of opposing birds in trees, in this case doves with their beaks linked by a row of beads, frame a mounted soldier in modern uniform, carrying a rifle. The doves are a religious motif from the Middle Ages: the soldier, all too modern.

PLATE 73: **ROSE KARABAGH**

4'7" x 9'6"

Dated 1905 and Inscribed
INSCRIPTION **1905. TIV. SE: S:O / S:VO N:VO H:A J:A S:A**

In proportion, heaviness of weave, color choice and over-all design this rug is typical of the "rose-patterned" Armenian Karabaghs woven about the turn of the century (cf. Plate 74). This handsome example is a little unusual in that a vase design has been chosen, and the field is filled with a scattering of Armenian initials, woven in pairs.

A similar handled vase is depicted in Plate 102 below, an Armenian rug from Feridun in central Iran, and a similar but handleless vase has been seen in Plate 59, a Karabagh dated 1899. In this rug the vase motif is combined with the double branching line seen more clearly in Plate 94, a rug from Khoy. Here the upper branch has been woven in such a deep blue it is almost invisible against the dark brown field. It is nevertheless an integral part of the design and helps link this rug stylistically with the other examples mentioned.

PLATE 73

ROSE KARABAGH    4'7" x 9'6"
Dated 1905 and Inscribed

COLORS:  Rose red, dark brown, pink, gold, yellow, indigo.

WARP:    WOOL, IVORY, 2 STRANDS, Z-SPIN, S-PLY

WEFT:    WOOL, IVORY, 2 STRANDS, Z-SPIN S-PLY, 3 SHOOTS

PILE:    WOOL, 2 STRANDS, S-SPIN, Z-PLY

KNOT:    GHIORDES, 48/inch

EDGES:   ROUND, GOLD

ENDS:    KILIM FOLDED AND SEWN; FRINGE UNRAVELLED

## PLATE 74: **ROSE KARABAGH**

5'x 11'

Dated 1911

Inscription: **1911 TIV**

In this example both border and field have been given over entirely to the European rose design. A few realistically depicted birds are hidden among the roses which comprise the entire pattern of this rug. In a few places unfaded colors testify to the dazzling —possibly lurid — appearance this rug must have had in 1911. In this type of Armenian Karabagh the suppression of local design and color, in favor of European taste, is almost complete.

PLATE 74

ROSE KARABAGH   5'x 11'
Dated 1911

COLORS:   Dark brown, gold, yellow, rose, pink, aniline blue, purple, pink and green.

WARP:     WOOL, TAN, 3 STRANDS, S-SPIN, Z-PLY

WEFT:     WOOL, TAN AND NATURAL, 3 STRANDS, Z-SPIN, S-PLY, 2 SHOOTS

PILE:     WOOL, 2 STRANDS, S̀-SPIN, Z-PLY

KNOT:     GHIORDES, ca. 42/inch

EDGES:    FLAT, DARK BROWN

ENDS:     KILIM FOLDED AND SEWN

PLATE 75: **ROSE KARABAGH**
3'6" x 7'4"   Dated 1931 and Inscribed
INSCRIPTION: **1931 TIV. SOKHAGZHAN**

PLATE 76: **ROSE KARABAGH**
3'6" x 6'5"   Dated 1938 and Inscribed
INSCRIPTION: **1938 TIV H GH + S A M I G K GH**

These rugs so resemble each other it is hard to believe that they were not made by
the same weaver. The chief difference is that the later example is knotted more finely,
and has the date drawn with greater finesse. Apart from a few obscure designs, and
repetitions of Armenian letters, the field of each rug is composed of well-executed
interpretations of the European rose design. Plate 76 is remarkable for its depth of pile,
fineness of weave and color and remarkable state of preservation. The letters scattered
about the columns of European-style roses may be signature initials, or they may have
a personal coded meaning.

PLATE 75                  PLATE 76

## PLATE 75: ROSE KARABAGH    3'6" x 7'4"
Dated 1931 and Inscribed

COLORS:   Dark brown, maroon, henna, pink, dark blue, green, ivory, black.

WARP:       WOOL, NATURAL TAN, 2 STRANDS, Z-SPIN, S-PLY

WEFT:        WOOL, PINK, IVORY AND GOLD, 1 STRAND, Z-SPIN, S-PLY,
              2 SHOOTS

PILE:         WOOL, 2 STRANDS, S-SPIN, Z-PLY

KNOT:       GHIORDES, ca. 42/inch

EDGES:    FLAT, TAN            ENDS:   KILIM FOLDED AND SEWN

## PLATE 76: ROSE KARABAGH    3'6" x 6'5"
Dated 1938 and Inscribed

COLORS:   Dark brown, maroon, henna, pink, dark and light blue, light green,
               ivory, black.

WARP:       WOOL, TAN AND BROWN, 3 STRANDS, Z-SPIN, S-PLY

WEFT:        WOOL, TAN AND PINK, 2 STRANDS, Z-SPIN, S-PLY, 2 SHOOTS

PILE:         WOOL, 2 STRANDS, S-SPIN, Z-PLY

KNOT:       GHIORDES, ca. 90/inch

EDGES:    FLAT, TAN       ENDS:   KILIM FOLDED AND SEWN

## PLATE 77: **ROSE KARABAGH**

4′4″ x 6′9″

Dated 1936
INSCRIPTION: **1936 TIV**

This is one of the latest examples we have in our collection of the all-over rose design, and it is one of the most handsome. Despite the use of sixteen different colors this rug looks rich rather than garish. The well-drawn flowers are shown in three different arrangements, two clusters and a wreath. Many flowers are used in addition to the popular rose. The sweeping leaf motifs in the border seem to be a return in style to the more primitive leaf forms seen in the border of Plate 73. It is likely that this rug was considered to be in the latest 'modern' style when it was woven. It must be remembered that a rug of this date is likely to have been composed by a professional designer.

PLATE 77

ROSE KARABAGH   4'4" x 6'9"
Dated 1936

COLORS: Maroon; henna; pink; dark, medium and light blue; turquoise; orange; gold;
yellow; dark, medium and light green; aniline blue; pink; purple.

WARP:    WOOL, TAN, 2 STRANDS, Z-SPIN, S-PLY

WEFT:    WOOL, TAN, 3 STRANDS, Z-SPIN, S-PLY, 3 SHOOTS

PILE:    WOOL, 2 STRANDS, S-SPIN, Z-PLY

KNOT:    GHIORDES, ca. 72/inch

EDGES:   FLAT, BLUE

ENDS:    KILIM FOLDED AND SEWN

## PLATE 78: ROSE KARABAGH

5' x 6'5"

ca. 1900, Inscribed
## INSCRIPTION: SIRANOUSH R.A.R.

The childish simplicity of this rug's design is in contrast to the regularity and polish of its weave. Some intention of copying the European rose design is clear, but the result is personal, whimsical and geometric. At the bottom the weaver has put her name and some initials. Geometric medallions alternate with stylized rose bushes in the border.

It should be pointed out that whereas this rug has more appeal to the Western eye than the polished examples immediately preceding, the weaver herself probably hoped to create something as exotic and rich as, for example, Plate 77, and emulated the European rose motif to the best of her ability.

PLATE 78

ROSE KARABAGH   5' x 6'5"
ca. 1900, Inscribed

COLORS:  Red, dark and light blue, dark brown, green, yellow, ivory, black.

WARP:    WOOL, TAN AND BROWN, 3 STRANDS, Z-SPIN, S-PLY

WEFT:    WOOL, TAN AND BROWN, 3 STRANDS, Z-SPIN, S-PLY, 2 SHOOTS

PILE:    WOOL, 2 STRANDS, S-SPIN, Z-PLY

KNOT:    GHIORDES, ca. 42/inch

EDGES:   FLAT, BROWN

ENDS:    KILIM, PLAITED AND FRINGED; KILIM FRINGED

PLATE 79: **ROSE KARABAGH** "MEDALLION DESIGN"

3'10" x 6'

Dated 1904 and Inscribed
INSCRIPTION: **KAGHO. KHARAVOV 1904**

Roses derived from European design form the border of this rug, framing a most
unusual collection of similarly borrowed medallions and flowers. Some Russian influence
may be inferred from the form of the weaver's last name. (Kagho is a familiar term for
"uncle.") The stylized blossoms above the inscription look as though they were drawn by
a different hand.

PLATE 79

ROSE KARABAGH "MEDALLION DESIGN"  3'10" x 6'
Dated 1904 and Inscribed

COLORS:  Red, henna, pink, gold, green, dark, medium and light blue,
           dark brown, ivory.

WARP:  WOOL, APRICOT, 3 STRANDS, Z-SPIN, S-PLY

WEFT:  WOOL, APRICOT, 2 STRANDS, Z-SPIN, S-PLY, 2 SHOOTS

PILE:  WOOL, 2 STRANDS, S-SPIN, Z-PLY

KNOT:  GHIORDES, ca. 72/inch

EDGES:  FLAT, HENNA

ENDS:  KILIM UNRAVELLED

PLATE 80: **ROSE KARABAGH** "MEDALLION DESIGN"

6' x 7'10"

Dated 1911 and Inscribed
INSCRIPTION **1911 AMI** (reversed)
                    **A/DF M/C** (gothic roman capitals)

The central medallions of this exotic rug are clearly of the same pattern as those in the preceding example, Plate 79. In most other respects this rug is singular, perhaps unique. Only the floral motifs on either side of the central medallions, and the meandering vine inner guard border with small blossoms, show any resemblance to other Karabagh rugs of the period.

For some reason, the weaver of this rug has commemorated the year 1911 with crowns, dragons, two representations of the double-headed eagle, and two representations of troikas dashing through the snow. Garlands and crowns isolate two sets of Gothic Roman initials in the field, A/DF and C/M. It seems most likely that a weaver with royalist enthusiasms has chosen to celebrate a marriage or similar happy event taking place in the Romanoff family, or perhaps among local nobility.

PLATE 80

ROSE KARABAGH "MEDALLION DESIGN"   6' x 7'10"
Dated 1911 and Inscribed

COLORS:   Henna, red, dark blue, dark green, black, pink, orange, aniline purple.

WARP:     WOOL, BROWN AND NATURAL, 3 STRANDS, Z-SPIN, S-PLY

WEFT:     WOOL, BROWN AND HENNA, 3 STRANDS, Z-SPIN, S-PLY, 2 SHOOTS

PILE:     WOOL, 2 STRANDS, Z-SPIN, S-PLY

KNOT:     GHIORDES, 54/inch

EDGES:    FLAT, MULTI-COLOR

ENDS:     FRINGED PLAIT; KILIM WITH FRINGE

## PLATE 81: **PICTORIAL KARABAGH**
4'3" x 18'8"   Dated 1904 and Inscribed
INSCRIPTION: **I.M.SH. 1904 AMI**

## PLATE 82: **PICTORIAL KARABAGH**
4' x 8'9"   c. 1900

Plate 81 is unusual in its restraint. The weaver, whose initials appear with the date, has made no attempt to intersperse her own fancies and crude drawings. The serious dogs appear very much as they must have on the European textile the weaver was copying; they are framed by a single border of roses, also made in a straight-forward realistic manner. The glorious henna-red of the field is in rich contrast to the faded chemical colors used for much of the pattern.

Although Plate 82 is not inscribed, it is included because of its close relationship with the previous, inscribed example. Unlike the first example, it mixes native folk-art motifs with the stylized pattern being copied. The horizontally placed dogs and horses are obvious copies from a European textile, but the vertical plane confusingly mixes in medallions, flowers, goats, chickens, roosters and booted men. These were added by the weaver on whim as her work progressed.

PLATE 81

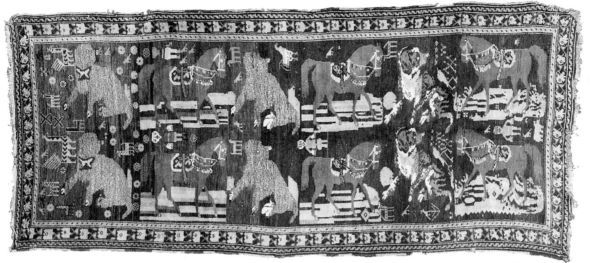

PLATE 82

PLATE 81: PICTORIAL KARABAGH    4'3" x 18'8"
Dated 1904 and Inscribed
COLORS:   Henna, maroon, dark and medium blue, dark green, dark brown, tan,
          orange, yellow, ivory, aniline purple, green and pink.

WARP:     WOOL, BROWN AND TAN, 3 STRANDS, Z-SPIN, S-PLY

WEFT:     WOOL, BROWN, 1 STRAND, Z-SPIN, S-PLY, 3 SHOOTS

PILE:     WOOL, 2 STRANDS, S-SPIN, Z-PLY

KNOT:     GHIORDES, ca. 63/inch

EDGES:    FLAT, DARK BROWN      ENDS:  PLAITED; KILIM

PLATE 82: PICTORIAL KARABAGH    4' x 8'9"
c. 1900
COLORS:   Henna, wine, dark brown, ivory, gold, tan, purple, light green, pink,
          orange, grey.

WARP:     WOOL, ORANGE AND BROWN, 3 STRANDS, Z-SPIN, S-PLY

WEFT:     WOOL AND COTTON, RED AND WHITE, 2 STRANDS, Z-SPIN, S-PLY, 2
          SHOOTS

PILE:     WOOL, 2 STRANDS, S-SPIN, Z-PLY

KNOT:     GHIORDES, ca. 54/inch

EDGES:    FLAT, MULTI-COLOR      ENDS:  KILIM WITH FRINGE

## PLATE 83: **PICTORIAL KARABAGH**

4'3" x 8'6"

Dated May 15, 1912 and Inscribed
INSCRIPTION: **1912 TIV, MAY 15 AROUSIAG M.E.**

A typically Russian Troika dashes across this rug, carrying a driver and two passengers. The wild eyes of the horses are made more staring by highlights of bright white cotton. As was the case in Plate 82, the Troika picture, running horizontally, has been copied by rote while spontaneous products of the weaver's fancy, woven vertically, intersect with the main pattern. This confusion of images adds to the overall sense of alarm which the rug conveys. The vertical images include many small geometric figures, human figures (including a man with a fez, moustache and long belted coat), primitive reindeer, an interpretation of the double-headed eagle, small birds, a tree of life and an ornately drawn rococo medallion. The inscription is most likely an obituary, for Arousiag (Venus) deceased (merrnil).

PLATE 83

## PICTORIAL KARABAGH   4'3" x 8'6"
Dated May 15, 1912 and Inscribed

COLORS:  Henna, dusty pink, medium and light blue, light green, yellow, dark and light brown, ivory, natural cotton.

WARP:    WOOL, TAN AND BROWN, 3 STRANDS, Z-SPIN, S-PLY

WEFT:    WOOL, TAN, 3 STRANDS, Z-SPIN, S-PLY, 2 SHOOTS

PILE:    WOOL, 2 STRANDS, S-SPIN, Z-PLY

KNOT:    GHIORDES, ca. 64/inch

EDGES:    FLAT, TAN

ENDS:    KILIM PLAITED; KILIM FRINGED

## PLATE 84: **PICTORIAL KARABAGH**

4'7" x 6'10"

Dated Jan. 4 1929 and Inscribed
INSCRIPTION: **19 1/4 29 TIV. A.V.**

This rug and the garland design following (Plate 85) are similar on many points and each
is a classic example of the European style in Armenian weaving which flourished from
about 1925-1939. There is absolutely nothing Armenian about the central design in
this rug, it is simply a remarkably skilled copy of a European textile, most probably a
machine-woven tapestry from Belgium. The skill with which Armenian weavers learned
to copy such designs was later put to good use by Soviet industry, with the production of
knotted-pile carpet portraits of prominent statesmen. It is possible that the inscription in
this case is less a commemorative than the signature of a proud and accomplished weaver.

PLATE 84

## PICTORIAL KARABAGH    4'7" x 6'10"
Dated Jan. 4 1929 and Inscribed

COLORS:  Wine, henna, aniline blue, gold, yellow, green, black, ivory, tan, pink, orange.

WARP:     WOOL, NATURAL AND BROWN, 3 STRANDS, Z-SPIN, S-PLY

WEFT:      WOOL, NATURAL 3 STRANDS, Z-SPIN, S-PLY, 2 SHOOTS

PILE:       WOOL, 2 STRANDS, Z-SPIN, S-PLY

KNOT:      GHIORDES, 49/inch

EDGES:     FLAT, DARK BROWN

ENDS:      UNRAVELLED KILIM; KILIM FOLDED AND SEWN

## PLATE 85: **ROSE KARABAGH**

4'4" x 7'4"

Dated 1925 and Inscribed
INSCRIPTION: **1925 TIV B.A.**

Since choosing the plates for this book, we have acquired an Armenian rug from Feridun in central Iran similar in size and design and date of completion, but different in color. Another similar Armenian rug from Feridun has been seen by us in a private collection in Europe. Apparently this striking heraldic design achieved widespread popularity among Armenian weavers in the 1920's.

The design is a combination of traditional and modern elements. A formally outlined medallion encloses a naturalistic wreath, drawn in a manner reminiscent of the flowers in Plate 77. Another attempt at formality can be seen in the stepped motif isolating the floral corners from the open red field. Again, as in Plate 77, a leaf design is used for the outer border.

PLATE 85

ROSE KARABAGH    4'4" x 7'4"
Dated 1925 and Inscribed

COLORS:  Red-brown, red, indigo, abrashed green, black, tan, ivory, aubergine, orange,
         yellow, pink.

WARP:    WOOL, TAN, 3 STRANDS, Z-SPIN, S-PLY

WEFT:    WOOL TAN, 2 STRANDS, Z-SPIN, S-PLY

PILE:    WOOL, 2 STRANDS, S-SPIN, Z-PLY

KNOT:    GHIORDES 48/INCH

EDGES:   ROUND, 3 CORDS, RED-BROWN

ENDS:    SELF-BRAID, SELF FRINGE

PLATE 86: **PICTORIAL KARABAGH**

4' x 5'8"

Dated Apr. 9, 1929
INSCRIPTION: **1992 TIV AB. 9**

A soldier in modern uniform, carrying a rifle, rides horseback across this rug. The traditionally stylized trees, topped with pairs of facing birds, make an incongruous frame; confronted pairs of birds, their beaks linked by scarves or strings of beads, are a classic motif in the Persian and Armenian decorative arts of antiquity. A crudely patched hole has marred the inscription, which reveals an illiterate weaver's attempt to render an important date. The brilliant color and folk-art motifs make a strange backdrop for the serious-looking Soviet Armenian horseman.

PLATE 86

## PICTORIAL KARABAGH   4' x 5'8"
Dated Apr. 9, 1929

COLORS:   Dark and medium red, dark brown, medium blue, chestnut, gold, ivory,
aniline green and purple.

WARP:     WOOL, WHITE, 3 STRANDS, Z-SPIN, S-PLY

WEFT:     WOOL, WHITE AND RED, 3 STRANDS, Z-SPIN, S-PLY, 2 SHOOTS

PILE:     WOOL, 2 STRANDS, S-SPIN, Z-PLY

KNOT:     GHIORDES, ca. 72/inch

EDGES:    FLAT, CHESTNUT

ENDS:      KILIM FOLDED AND SEWN; KILIM FRINGED

ANATOLIA 1862 *(Engraving)*

FERIDUN 1972 *(Photograph)*

## ARMENIAN PEASANT WOMEN

Two peasant women a century apart in time and miles apart in space: and yet so close. Each covers her head and mouth in the same fashion, wears the same type of work-apron to protect her jacket and skirt; each spins by drop-spindle the wool for her future rug.

# V: ARMENIAN RUGS OF THE DIASPORA

We have seen that Greater Armenia included the district surrounding Lake Urmia, that part of north-west Iran known as Moghan and Karadagh. Additional Armenian settlements in modern Iran extend along the western borders into Kurdistan as far as Sanandaj and Hamadan. When Shah Abbas the Great transported thousands of Armenians to Isfahan, they settled in the suburb of New Julfa. It is not surprising that Armenian villages are dotted along the road leading from Hamadan to Isfahan. The most notable concentration occurs in the district of Feridun about 100 miles north-west of Isfahan, and includes the villages of Gulpaygan and Buleran.

Central Asia lies as close to Greater Armenia as Iran. The Caspian Sea that separates the Caucasus from the steppes of Asia is more a highway than a barrier, filled with commercial shipping. Armenian merchants and travellers in Asia have been a commonplace since the days of the Armeno-Mongol alliance. Indeed, all across Asia Armenians settled and built churches. (Armenians were welcomed to northern India by the Moghul court as early as the 16th century, and by 1813 there was an Armenian church in Rangoon.) It is not surprising that Asiatic motifs occur in some Armenian rugs.

The Armenian presence in Central Asia was strengthened during the 18th century by Nadir Shah when he moved a population of Armenians from Nakchivan to Meshed. Meshed is the chief market-town for Eastern Iran, the center for trade with Afghanistan, the last stop on the road to Herat. It is a center for Turkoman culture as well as Persian. Consider Plate 104. This rug is inscribed as being the property of Mirza Sarukhaniantz. "Sarukh" could refer to the town of Sarakhs, on the border of Iran and Afghanistan near Meshed, or to the Sarukh Turkoman tribe. "Mirza" is a contraction of the old term Emir-zadeh (sons of the Emir), and is not a term used by Armenians except those attached to the Moghul court.

When this rug was located in Turkey, the Armenian inscription had been entirely inked out. Goods from Central Asia are often brought to market in Turkey by pilgrims financing their travels. It is impossible to say how long this piece has carried its Armenian secret. It is a beautiful and enigmatic rug, the only one of its kind known.

PLATE 87: **MOGHAN** "GUL DESIGN"
5'2" x 12'9"   Dated 1928 and Inscribed
INSCRIPTION: unclear

PLATE 88: **MOGHAN** "GUL DESIGN"
4'5" x 7'8"   Dated Apr. 1, 1900
INSCRIPTION: **I. 1900 AMI 1 APRLI**

From Dasht-i-Moghan, in the northern Azerbaijan, come these rugs with repeated
rows of medallions. In Plate 87, the date is written in ornate Armenian numerals first,
followed by the same year (i.e., the Christian calendar year) in Arabic numerals more
crudely drawn. The inscription is hard to interpret, and indeed may be the result of an
illiterate weaver's attempt to copy writing she did not understand. The shades of red
and blue are typically Armenian.

Where Plate 87 has a Persian feeling in its complexity of design and scale of pattern,
Plate 88 has the simpler, bolder feeling of a central Caucasian rug. The terse inscription
is beautifully drawn, followed by a band of random pattern. Other discontinuous designs
puncuate the field.

PLATE 87

PLATE 88

## PLATE 87: MOGHAN "GUL DESIGN"   5'2" x 12'9"
Dated 1928 and Inscribed

COLORS:  Henna, bright red, dark and light blue, gold, green-gold, aniline pink and
purple, ivory, dark brown, black.

WARP:     WOOL, BROWN AND IVORY, 4 STRANDS, Z-SPIN, S-PLY

WEFT:      WOOL, BROWN AND TAN, 2 STRANDS, Z-SPIN, S-PLY, 3 SHOOTS

PILE:        WOOL, 2 STRANDS, S-SPIN, Z-PLY

KNOT:      GHIORDES, ca. 56/inch

EDGES:     FLAT, MULTI-COLOR     ENDS:  KILIM, PLAIT AND FRINGE;
KILIM AND FRINGE


## PLATE 88: MOGHAN "GUL DESIGN"   4'5" x 7'8"
Dated Apr. 1, 1900

COLORS:  Henna, dark and light blue, green, gold, ivory, dark brown, black, coral.

WARP:     WOOL, NATURAL AND BROWN, 3 STRANDS, Z-SPIN, S-PLY

WEFT:      WOOL, FADED ORANGE, 2 STRANDS, Z-SPIN, S-PLY, 2 SHOOTS

PILE:        WOOL, 2 STRANDS, Z-SPIN, S-PLY

KNOT:      GHIORDES, 64/inch

EDGES:     FLAT, MULTI-COLOR     ENDS:  KILIM FOLDED AND SEWN (BOTH)

PREVIOUSLY PUBLISHED: (87) The Gregorian Collection Of Armenian Rugs
(Dartmouth); Armenian Rugs — The Gregorian Collection (Michigan)

## PLATE 89: **AZERBAIJAN** *VISHAPAGORG* "CLOUDBAND DESIGN"

4'1" x 7'9"

Dated 18110 and Inscribed
INSCRIPTION: **18110** (blue)
            **YE L N** (ivory)

The wide field and narrow rosette border seen here are typical of some Karabagh rugs, most notably the so-called "eagle" design rugs, a variant of the "dragon" design. This rug combines the ancient patterns of Karabagh with the wool, colors and finish typical of the Moghan district, on the Persian side of the border.

The weaver of this rug does not seem to have been completely dedicated to this design: the medallions differ in size and the *Vishap* vary in many particulars. There is also great freedom in the choice of subsidiary ornament, and liberties are taken with the motifs which support the central *Vishap*. Compare this to the classic "cloudband" *Vishapagorg* rugs shown in Plates 32-36.

PLATE 89

AZERBAIJAN *VISHAPAGORG* "CLOUDBAND DESIGN"   4'1" x 7'9"
Dated 18110 and Inscribed

COLORS: Red, henna, dark and light blue, yellow, dark and light green, dark brown, ivory.

WARP:    WOOL, TAN AND BROWN, 3 STRANDS, Z-SPIN, S-PLY

WEFT:    WOOL, TAN AND BROWN, 2 STRANDS, Z-SPIN, S-PLY, 2 SHOOTS

PILE:    WOOL, 2 STRANDS, S-SPIN, Z-PLY

KNOT:    GHIORDES, ca. 35/inch

EDGES:   FLAT, MULTI-COLOR

ENDS:    KILIM FOLDED AND SEWN; UNRAVELLED

## PLATE 90: **KARADAGH *VISHAPAGORG*** "SUNBURST DESIGN"

3'9" x 6'3"

Dated Mar. 10, 1889
INSCRIPTION: **18 3/10 89 AMI**

This variation on the *Vishapagorg* design is often called 'sunburst' by western critics. The *Vishap* or S-shaped dragon appears in very stylized form, woven in pairs to surround the center of each medallion. The medallion as a whole is a variation on the motif also known as "Leshgi star" (Plates 91 and 92). As with the "star" design, the basic theme is of two crosses superimposed, a diagonal one on top of a squared one, much in the manner of the Union Jack.

In the "sunburst" design the diagonal elements become attentuated while the vertical axis takes primary importance. In the Kars rug shown in Plate 3 above the diagonal elements have actually disappeared. In the "star" design the vertical and horizontal members become forked, while the diagonal elements become pointed.

This example has the heavy-wefted simple style we associate with Karadagh and Dasht-i-Moghan, Caucasian in appearance but Persian in texture and color. Apparently the decision to make this rug a commemorative piece was sudden, for the inscription interrupts the final medallion and it seems the rug was finished in haste, although the commemorative date is beautifully drawn. The "cossack-style" riders standing on horseback enliven the usual collection of birds, goats and random medallions filling the field.

PLATE 90

KARADAGH *VISHAPAGORG* "SUNBURST DESIGN"    3'9" x 6'3"
Dated Mar. 10, 1889

COLORS:  Henna, dark and light blue, gold, yellow, ivory, dark brown, aniline purple.

WARP:    WOOL, NATURAL, 3 STRANDS, Z-SPIN, S-PLY

WEFT:    WOOL, BROWN AND TAN, 2 STRANDS, Z-SPIN, S-PLY, 2 SHOOTS

PILE:    WOOL, 2 STRANDS, S-SPIN, Z-PLY

KNOT:    GHIORDES, ca. 48/inch

EDGES:   MISSING

ENDS:    UNRAVELLED

PREVIOUSLY PUBLISHED: Armenian Rugs — The Gregorian Collection (Michigan)

PLATE 91: **AZERBAIJAN** "LESHGI STAR DESIGN"
4'9" x 9'6"   Dated 1900 and Inscribed
INSCRIPTION: **1900 M.**


PLATE 92: **AZERBAIJAN** "LESHGI STAR DESIGN"
4'3" x 8'5"   Dated 1905 and Inscribed
INSCRIPTION: **1905 TIV M.T.** (ivory)
              **AMI TIV AGH** (red, random)

These are traditional Azerbaijani rugs in color, proportion and solidity of weave. Both use the "Leshgi Star," more typical of the Shemakha district in the Caucasus. Plate 91 is a rug which shows the effects of having been buried for safe-keeping during a period of trouble. Despite the damage the fabric is still strong and resilient. Goats, medallions and tiny equilateral crosses fill the available field.

Plate 92 is similar in weave, but bolder and more open in design. Many Armenian letters, very well drawn, are scattered along the edges of the field, woven in red. Some seem to refer to dating (TIV, AMI) while the reference to salt (AGH) seems to imply a baptism. Other typically Armenian touches include the pairs of opposing birds.

The "Leshgi Star" pattern is described above in reference to Plates 2 and 30.

PLATE 91                        PLATE 92

## PLATE 91: AZERBAIJAN "LESHGI STAR DESIGN"    4'9" x 9'6"
Dated 1900 and Inscribed

COLORS:  Henna, coral, rose, gold, dark and medium blue, teal, green, dark brown,
           ivory.

WARP:    WOOL, TAN, 3 STRANDS, Z-SPIN, S-PLY

WEFT:    WOOL, BROWN, RED AND TAN, 2 STRANDS, Z-SPIN, S-PLY,
           2 SHOOTS

PILE:    WOOL, 2 STRANDS, S-SPIN, Z-PLY

KNOT:    GHIORDES, ca. 54/inch

EDGES:   FLAT, DARK BROWN     ENDS:  KILIM WITH PLAIT; KILIM FRINGED

## PLATE 92: AZERBAIJAN "LESHGI STAR DESIGN"    4'3" x 8'5"
Dated 1905 and Inscribed

COLORS:  Henna, coral, gold, dark and medium blue, abrashed green, dark brown,
           ivory, aniline orange.

WARP:    WOOL, BROWN AND NATURAL, 3 STRANDS, Z-SPIN, S-PLY

WEFT:    WOOL, TAN, 2 STRANDS, Z-SPIN, S-PLY, 2 SHOOTS

PILE:    WOOL, 2 STRANDS, S-SPIN, Z-PLY

KNOT:    GHIORDES, ca. 49/inch

EDGES:   FLAT, GOLD     ENDS:  KILIM FOLDED AND SEWN; UNRAVELLED

## PLATE 93: **KHOY** "FEREGHAN DESIGN"

5' x 10'9"

Dated 1887
INSCRIPTION: **1887 AMI**

This rug offers an interpretation of the classic Fereghan pattern, a repeated blossom and leaf motif. This is one of the most beloved designs of the Azerbaijan region. The round blossom is popularly held to represent the world, while the leaves that curl around it are the fishes which circle the earth with day and night. Hence the popular term "fish-pattern" for rugs using this design.

This example is unlike most Fereghan patterned rugs in its choice of border. Normally, a "turtle" border such as the ones in Plates 98 and 99 is chosen. Like many Azerbaijani rugs, this one combines a cotton weft and edging with an otherwise all-wool construction. Khoy is a town in the northern Azerbaijan which had a large Armenian population before the First World War.

PLATE 93

KHOY "FEREGHAN DESIGN"   5' x 10'9"
Dated 1887

COLORS: Red, rose, pink, gold, abrashed medium blue, medium green, sienna and dark brown, black, ivory.

WARP:   WOOL, BROWN AND NATURAL, 3 STRANDS, Z-SPIN, S-PLY

WEFT:   COTTON, NATURAL, 2 STRANDS, 2 SHOOTS

PILE:   WOOL, 2 STRANDS, S-SPIN, Z-PLY

KNOT:   GHIORDES, ca. 56/inch

EDGES:  FLAT, NATURAL COTTON

ENDS:   REWOVEN AND OVERCAST; FRINGED

PREVIOUSLY PUBLISHED: The Gregorian Collection Of Armenian Rugs (Dartmouth); Armenian Rugs — The Gregorian Collection (Michigan)

## PLATE 94: **KHOY** "BRANCHING FLOWER DESIGN"

5' x 12'2"

### Dated 1882 and Inscribed
### INSCRIPTION: **1882 GR.IKIDOV**

This fascinating rug uses a pattern more common to Central Asia than the Near East, a stylized, repetitive design made up of flowering pomegranates. Many rugs of similar design can be found in the regions around Samarkand and Khotan. The strong blues and yellows of this rug are also Asiatic in feeling. But this is hardly surprising since the Azerbaijan district has strong cultural and linguistic links with Turkestan. The Azeri Turks are closer to their Asiatic roots than are the Turks of Anatolia; spoken Azeri is very similar to the language of Turkestan, and very different from that of Istanbul. Historically, the Armenians of the Azerbaijan enjoyed a friendly rapport with their Azeri Turk neighbors, and there was continual cultural exchange.

PLATE 94

KHOY "BRANCHING FLOWER DESIGN"   5' x 12'2"
Dated 1882 and Inscribed

COLORS:   Henna, red, medium blue, abrashed green, gold, magenta, rose-pink, dark and
              light brown, black, ivory.

WARP:     WOOL, IVORY AND TAN, 2 STRANDS, Z-SPIN, S-PLY

WEFT:      WOOL, IVORY AND TAN, 2 STRANDS, Z-SPIN, S-PLY, 2 SHOOTS

PILE:        WOOL, 2 STRANDS, Z-SPIN, S-PLY

KNOT:      GHIORDES, ca. 81/inch

EDGES:     FLAT, RED

ENDS:       NARROW KILIM

PREVIOUSLY PUBLISHED: The Gregorian Collection Of Armenian Rugs (Dartmouth);
Armenian Rugs — The Gregorian Collection (Michigan)

PLATE 95: **AZERBAIJAN** "BRANCHING FLOWER DESIGN"

4'6" x 7'10"

Dated May 10, 1907 and Inscribed
INSCRIPTION: **KHANRM. IVOENTS 19 5/x 07**

This repeated flowering plant motif is typical of much village weaving in the
Dasht-i-Moghan and Karadagh region. The rich, deep colors are also native to the
area. In addition to the name and date, this weaver has added a few variant floral
motifs and several small birds to the design along the edges of the field. This is a
rug with stronger Caucasian ties than Persian ones, despite its provenance.

PLATE 95

AZERBAIJAN "BRANCHING FLOWER DESIGN"   4'6" x 7'10"
Dated May 10, 1907 and Inscribed

COLORS:  Abrashed rose-red, pink, dark green, abrashed blue, dark brown, ivory.

WARP:     WOOL, TAN AND BROWN, 3 STRANDS, Z-SPIN, S-PLY

WEFT:      WOOL, TAN AND RED, 2 STRANDS, Z-SPIN, S-PLY, 2 SHOOTS

PILE:       WOOL, 2 STRANDS, S-SPIN, Z-PLY

KNOT:      GHIORDES, ca. 42/inch

EDGES:    FLAT, ROSE

ENDS:      PLAITED

PLATE 96: **MAKU** "BRANCHING FLOWER DESIGN"

*4' x 7'6"*

Dated 1888 and Inscribed

INSCRIPTION: garbled (red)
        **SATENI G IANOS** (ivory), (top line reversed)
        **1888 TIV HAGOP TSAGHO** (V)

Maku is an important town for Armenians, since it is the location of the ancient church of St. Thaddeus, an object of yearly pilgrimage. This charming rug intersperses people, animals and crosses within a repetitive geometric design. An attempt at a word is made in the center, marked by a cross in ivory; the top inscription is clearer though obviously illiterate, since the top line is woven in mirror writing. Satenig and Hagop are common Armenian names, female and male respectively; Tsagho is a familiar diminutive. The deep blues and oranges are classic tones for this area.

PLATE 96

## MAKU "BRANCHING FLOWER DESIGN"   4' x 7'6"
Dated 1888 and Inscribed

COLORS:  Magenta, henna, orange, natural, dark and abrashed medium brown, dark
and abrashed medium blue, ivory.

WARP:    WOOL, BROWN AND TAN, 3 STRANDS, Z-SPIN, S-PLY

WEFT:    WOOL, BROWN AND TAN, 3 STRANDS, Z-SPIN, S-PLY, 3 SHOOTS

PILE:    WOOL, 2 STRANDS, S-SPIN, Z-PLY

KNOT:    GHIORDES, ca. 49/inch

EDGES:   FLAT, MAGENTA

ENDS:    PLAITED

## PLATE 97: **KARADAGH** "TREE OF LIFE DESIGN"

4' x 6'8"

Dated 1931 and Inscribed

INSCRIPTION:**SHOUSHIK** (blue)
**1931 TIV SHOUSHIK BADALI** (ivory)

Another thick-napped, heavy-wefted rug,this time showing the influence of Kurdish or village Bidjar weaving. Variations of this pattern, showing deer browsing on trees or potted plants, were common much earlier, about the turn of the century. Some Bachtiari rugs use a similar design. In this version, the tree grows like a plant from an ornate vase; birds are perched in the twigs, deer browse on some of the leaves and heraldic lions are stretched out along the branches. These are typically Persian lions, an incomplete version of the classic "lion and sun" motif.

The deep, sombre colors are traditional to Karadagh. The almost unbordered effect, created by tiny guard borders and an unusually large-patterned main border, is usually seen only in certain village Bidjar rugs. The Armenian weaver has signed her name twice, once running vertically along the upper left of the field, and again, with more confidence, in the final inscription.

PLATE 97

KARADAGH "TREE OF LIFE DESIGN"   4' x 6'8"
Dated 1931 and Inscribed

COLORS:   Dark and medium brown, tan, magenta, rose, dark and light blue, green,
          gold, yellow, ivory.

WARP:     WOOL, BROWN & TAN, 3 STRANDS, Z-SPIN, S-PLY

WEFT:     WOOL, BROWN, 3 STRANDS, Z-SPIN, S-PLY, 2 SHOOTS

PILE:     WOOL, 2 STRANDS, Z-SPIN, S-PLY

KNOT:     SENNA, GHIORDES, ca. 48/inch

EDGES:    FLAT, LIGHT BROWN

ENDS:     KILIM FOLDED AND SEWN; KILIM FRINGED

PLATE 98: **AZERBAIJAN** "FEREGHAN DESIGN"
4'7" x 7'10"   Dated 1926 and Inscribed
INSCRIPTION: **1926 V.A.**


PLATE 99: **AZERBAIJAN** "FEREGHAN DESIGN"
5'4" x 8'10"   Dated 1927 and Inscribed
INSCRIPTION: **1927 AMI ARGHOV**

The open-field Fereghan design, large-scale turtle border and heavy-wefted weave give these rugs the appearance of those woven in Sanandaj, in Kurdistan. The color scheme is similar to that seen in many Armenian Karabaghs, however, and the neat dates and lettering leave no doubt of the weaver's nationality. Many Armenians resident in the Azerbaijan have close family ties with the Karabagh region, and this is a good example of a rug displaying characteristics of both sides of the border. It is interesting to note that these two rugs, clearly from the same village if not from the same family, came into our collection from different sources at two different times. Their chief difference lies in the sun-fading suffered by Plate 98.

PLATE 98                                  PLATE 99

## PLATE 98: AZERBAIJAN "FEREGHAN DESIGN"    4'7" x 7'10"
Dated 1926 and Inscribed

COLORS:   Magenta, henna, orange, pink, abrashed blue, abrashed green,
                 dark brown, ivory.

WARP:      WOOL, TAN, 3 STRANDS, Z-SPIN, S-PLY

WEFT:       WOOL, TAN AND YELLOW, Z-SPIN, S-PLY, 2 SHOOTS

PILE:        WOOL, 2 STRANDS, S-SPIN, Z-PLY

KNOT:      GHIORDES, 72/inch

EDGES:     FLAT, YELLOW      ENDS:  KILIM

## PLATE 99: AZERBAIJAN "FEREGHAN DESIGN"    5'4" x 8'10"
Dated 1927 and Inscribed

COLORS:   Magenta, henna, orange, pink, abrashed blue, abrashed green, yellow,
                 brown, ivory.

WARP:      WOOL, TAN, 3 STRANDS, Z-SPIN, S-PLY

WEFT:       TAN WOOL AND IVORY COTTON, 2 STRANDS, Z-SPIN, S-PLY,
                 2 SHOOTS

PILE:        WOOL, 2 STRANDS, S-SPIN, Z-PLY

KNOT:      GHIORDES, 72/inch

EDGES:     ROUND, YELLOW     ENDS:  KILIM FOLDED AND SEWN (BOTH)

PLATE 100: **AZERBAIJAN** "THREE MEDALLION DESIGN"

4'8" x 8'6"

Dated Oct. 20, 1928 and Inscribed
INSCRIPTION: **1928 TIV OCT 20th GEGHETSIGH G.**

A magnificent rug in excellent condition. *Geghetsigh* means 'Beautiful' and is sometimes used as a girl's name. The simple, rhythmic pattern and deep, rich color makes this an impressive masterwork for some obscure Armenian villager. The rug is in the tradition of weaving done in the Kurdish area near Souj-Boulak. The initial G could be for gin, "bride."

Since compiling the plates for this book, we have added another similar rug to our collection, also dated from the 1920's. It is interesting to see how these Armenian rugs from the Persian side of the border recall several different Caucasian elements, both Kazak and Karabagh yet unite them in a Persian manner. The red band outlining the medallions is reminiscent of the "saw-tooth medallion" Karabagh style, while the outlining detail within the medallions is similar to the *"Khatchk'ar"* Kazaks.

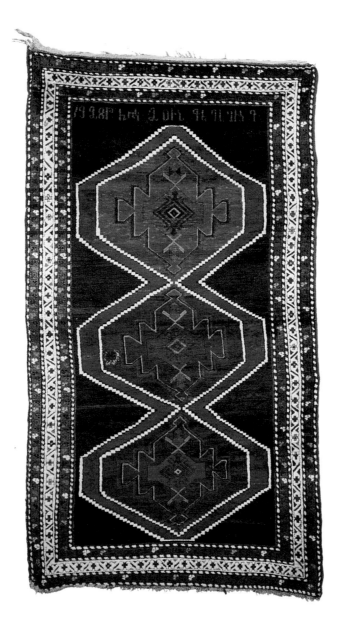

PLATE 100

AZERBAIJAN "THREE MEDALLION DESIGN"    4'8" x 8'6"
Dated Oct. 20, 1928 and Inscribed

COLORS:  Henna, coral, dark blue, abrashed medium blue, dark green, dark brown, tan, ivory.

WARP:    WOOL, NATURAL AND LIGHT BROWN, 3 STRANDS, Z-SPIN, S-PLY

WEFT:    WOOL, RED AND BROWN, 2 STRANDS, Z-SPIN, S-PLY, 1 SHOOT

PILE:    WOOL, 2 STRANDS, Z-SPIN, S-PLY

KNOT:    GHIORDES, ca. 49/inch

EDGES:   FLAT, RED

ENDS:    KILIM AND PLAIT; KILIM FRINGED

PLATE 101: **FERIDUN** "NOUSH DESIGN"

5'10" x 9'

Dated 1868
INSCRIPTION: **1868**

The Armenians of Feridun are culturally isolated, both from Greater Armenia to
their north and from the Armenians of New Julfa to their south. Although Armenian
textiles from Feridun often show less Caucasian feeling than Armenian rugs from the
Azerbaijan, this dignified old rug is enlivened by an outer guard border more common to
Kazaks than Persian village-weaves. A note of eccentricity is struck by the single row of
potted plants which interrupts the design. On the edges of the field a woman is drawn
standing arms akimbo; above her is a small cross. The many irregularities of this piece
suggest a very simple village origin.

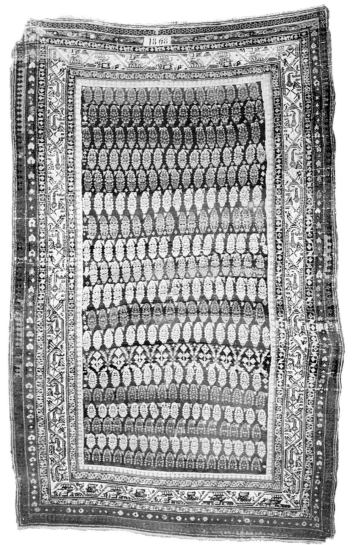

PLATE 101

FERIDUN "NOUSH DESIGN"   5'10" x 9'
Dated 1868

COLORS:  Henna, abrashed blue, yellow, green, black, white, brown, faded aniline
         purple, pink.

WARP:    WOOL, IVORY AND TAN, 2 STRANDS, Z-SPIN, S-PLY

WEFT:    WOOL, IVORY AND BROWN, 2 STRANDS, Z-SPIN, S-PLY, 1-2 SHOOTS

PILE:    WOOL, 2 STRANDS, Z-SPIN, S-PLY

KNOT:    GHIORDES, ca. 80/inch

EDGES:   FLAT, BROWN

ENDS:    WORN; FRINGED

PREVIOUSLY PUBLISHED: The Gregorian Collection Of Armenian Rugs (Dartmouth);
Weavers, Merchants and Kings (Fort Worth) Armenian Rugs — The Gregorian
Collection (Michigan)

## PLATE 102: **FERIDUN** "BRANCHING FLOWER DESIGN"

8'3" x 10'

### Dated 1921 and Inscribed
### INSCRIPTION: **IVAYEM'SH SERG VART 1921**

This large carpet in some ways resembles the Bachtiari carpets for which the region around Feridun is famous. It is firmer in construction than most similar Bachtiari rugs, however, and uses an all-wool construction. Most Twentieth Century Bachtiari rugs are on a cotton foundation.

A repeated vase motif is used. But compare the drawing in this large carpet to the branching flowers depicted in the rugs of Plates 94 and 97. In all three rugs the stem or vase branches out into a V with doubled arms. This stylized pattern is much more sophisticated than the cruder and more naturalistic flowering branches seen in Bachtiari carpets from the same area. Furthermore, the sides and handles of the vases are drawn in a serrated, s-shaped line recalling the ancient *Vishap* motif. In outline the vases are not unlike the medallions of the famed Gohar carpet, an Eighteenth Century rug pictured in Weavers, Merchants and Kings.

Unlike Bachtiari rugs, which often suffer from poorly designed border patterns, this rug is well framed by a triple border in the Kazak style. The letters and numbers of the inscription are beautifully formed, suggesting a literate weaver. The interruption of the design by the inscription and final border suggests that something forced the weaver to complete this rug a little sooner than intended. Serg Vart is "flower of the quince," a name.

PLATE 102

FERIDUN "BRANCHING FLOWER DESIGN"   8'3" x 10'
Dated 1921 and Inscribed

COLORS:  Red, dark and light blue, dark and medium green, black, dark brown,
         ivory, gold.

WARP:    WOOL, BROWN AND NATURAL, 2 STRANDS, S-SPIN, Z-PLY

WEFT:    WOOL, RED AND YELLOW, 2 STRANDS, S-SPIN, Z-PLY, 2 SHOOTS

PILE:    WOOL, 2 STRANDS, S-SPIN, Z-PLY

KNOT:    GHIORDES, ca. 42/inch

EDGES:   ROUND, DARK BLUE AND RED

ENDS:    PLAIT WITH FRINGE; KILIM WITH PLAITED FRINGE

PREVIOUSLY PUBLISHED: The Gregorian Collection Of Armenian Rugs (Dartmouth);
Armenian Rugs — The Gregorian Collection (Michigan)

PLATE 103: **FERIDUN** "AFSHAR DESIGN"

4'8" x 8'6"

Dated June 10, 1902 and Inscribed
INSCRIPTION: **This rug was woven June 10, 1902 by Tatos Davit Panosian**

This richly colored, heavy-textured rug recalls the red/blue coloring, leaf and star motifs of Afshar tribal weaving. It is from one of the villages of Feridun. Even the brown flat-weave at the ends, touched by a row of colored wool, is Afshar or Kurdish in character. The repetitive motif in the center appears to be a very stylized "branching flower," similar in outline to the rug in Plate 96, though much more finely knotted. Apart from the inscription there is little that is specifically Armenian about this rug.

PLATE 103

FERIDUN "AFSHAR DESIGN"   4'8" x 8'6"
Dated June 10, 1902 and Inscribed

COLORS:  Magenta, henna, melon, green-gold, dark green, abrashed blue, ivory, dark
         brown, black.

WARP:    WOOL, BROWN AND IVORY, 2 STRANDS, Z-SPIN, S-PLY

WEFT:    WOOL, BROWN, Z-SPIN, S-PLY, 1 SHOOT

PILE:    WOOL, 2 STRANDS, Z-SPIN, S-PLY

KNOT:    GHIORDES, ca. 120/inch

EDGES:   ROUND, BLACK

ENDS:    KILIM AND PLAITED FRINGE; KILIM & PLAIT


PREVIOUSLY PUBLISHED: Armenian Rugs — The Gregorian Collection (Michigan)

## PLATE 104: **TURKESTAN** "SALOR DESIGN"

5'2" x 7'7"

Dated 1888 and Inscribed

INSCRIPTION: **BADGANOUME MIRZA SAROUKHANIANTS**
                **1888 AMI**

At first glance this rug seems to be an excellent example of 19th century Turkoman weaving, of a type described by various authorities as Saryk, Salor or Tekke. Closer examination shows several anomalies in addition to the surprising inscription. The motifs chosen for the borders are common to Yomut carpets, but not to Salor/Tekke pieces; yet the weave and main design relate to the latter group. Stranger still is the lack of any additional design at the ends of the carpet: no apron of extra design beyond the borders; no luxuriant expanse of flat-weave. The narrow finishing band of kilim is in the Tekke style, but uses once more a motif preferred by the Yomut. (This same combination of main motif, border motifs and lack of apron can be seen in Plate 72 above, a delightfully primitive Karabagh woven in a Turkoman pattern.) The tiny four-dot crosses of the outer guard border are sometimes seen in Turkoman rugs, but are more common in Caucasian weaving. Finally there is the matter of field color, a true Armenian crimson, not the typical Turkoman madder-red or the aniline plum color used in late Tekke weaving.

We will never know the whole story behind this rug. The flawlessly formed Armenian inscription (which translates as "the absolute property of Mirza Saroukhanian, in the year 1888") is unlikely to be the work of a Turkoman tribal woman. Turkoman rugs woven before 1900 did not reflect a literate culture and did not carry dates or inscriptions. In issue 35 of HALI (summer 1987) a "giant Tekke" is described, inscribed in Russian and in Arabic and also dated to 1888. Much larger in size (12'10" x 34'2") and coarser in weave (132 knots/inch) it uses more colors, has conventional borders and aprons. On other points it is altogether similar both in appearance and technical analysis, although the inscriptions are crude, poorly formed and awkwardly placed. Even so, the two rugs share similar designs, dates and the oddity of being inscribed. That another inscribed Turkoman rug should be found, with its Russian/Arabic inscription so badly formed, makes the flawless and literate Armenian inscription on Plate 104 even more engimatic, even more indicative of an Armenian master-weaver.

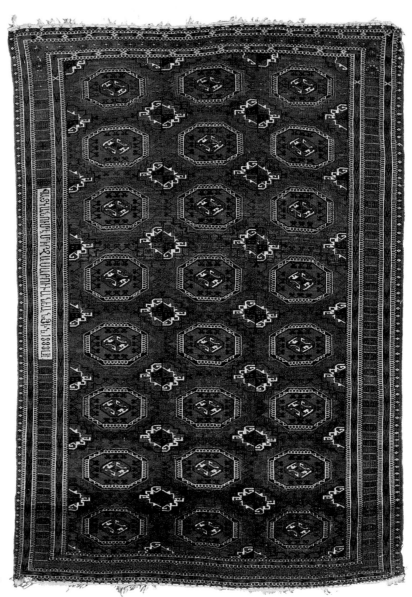

PLATE 104

TURKESTAN "SALOR DESIGN"   5'2" x 7'7"
Dated 1888 and Inscribed

COLORS:  Crimson, orange-red, dark blue, medium blue, ivory, dark brown.

WARP:    WOOL, IVORY, 2 STRANDS, Z-SPIN, S-PLY

WEFT:    WOOL, BROWN, 2 STRANDS, Z-SPIN, S-PLY, 2 SHOOTS

PILE:    WOOL, 2 STRANDS, Z-SPIN, S-PLY

KNOT:    SENNA, ca. 220/inch

EDGES:   ROUND, DARK BLUE

ENDS:    1" KILIM, EMBROIDERED

PREVIOUSLY PUBLISHED: The Gregorian Collection Of Armenian Rugs (Dartmouth);
Armenian Rugs — The Gregorian Collection (Michigan)

# AFTERWORD

Armenians have lived in western Anatolia and the southern Caucasus for at least 2500 years, at the crossroads of trade between East and West. For at least 1300 years, they have been noted for their miniature painting, sculpture and architecture. For at least 1000 years, they have been noted for their dyes and textiles.

Armenians are villagers: farmers, craftsmen, merchants. They are not exotic tribespeople with tents and camel-trappings and curious personal customs: the life they live has not inspired the anthropological excitement caused, for example, by study of the Yomut Turkoman or the Shah Sevan.

Unfortunately, for the cause of Armenian rugs, much of the western world's interest in oriental carpets has been impelled by a romantic enthusiasm for things Islamic. The products of Islamic history, scholarship and talent are phenomenal and well deserving of our study. But it is foolish of scholars to ignore or dismiss the contribution made by non-Islamic peoples living in what we have come to consider the Islamic world.

Only within the last ten years have groups of rugs woven by Armenians been published, discussed and examined. Search through any large library of oriental rug books, catalogues and periodicals: if you are persistant, you may find some trivial reference to Armenians as the possible weavers of rugs. For example, rugs noted as being inscribed in Armenian might be dismissed as having been woven to order by Islamic weavers for Armenian buyers. Even the famed "Gohar Carpet," a classic 17th/18th century inscribed dragon-rug known from photographs for decades, was considered by some experts a hoax until it was once more placed on public exhibition as part of "Weavers, Merchants and Kings."

This is hard for an unprejudiced new-comer to the world of oriental rugs to understand. A glance at the history of Anatolia and the southern Caucasus shows how different groups of Turkomans migrated westward into the territory of Byzantium, establishing settlements and military power in the countryside until finally, in the late 15th century, Constantinople itself fell to the Osmanli or "Ottoman" Turks. The land they conquered had been enriched for over 1000 years by Greek and Armenian Christian culture. A treasury of aesthetic riches lay open to the Turkic conquerors.

We can guess what type of rug the Turkomans were weaving at this time. Today in Central Asia, Turkomans are still weaving beautiful rugs of the type once called "Boukara" after the main point of collection and marketing. Turkoman rugs are handsome and highly prized by collectors, with repetitive medallions enclosed within geometric borders. Rugs resembling modern Afghan carpets are pictured in 14th century Sung Dynasty paintings of nomadic life in Chinese Turkestan; rugs quite similar in appearance can be seen in European painting of the 15th and 16th centuries, rugs presumably brought to Europe from the Ottoman Empire.

But there are other types of rugs shown in Renaissance paintings. Simple rugs with stylized animals, complex rugs with over-all interlocking motifs. Many represent a degree of sophistication in their design, the origins of which would be hard to explain if it were not for the Byzantine and Armenian designs extant in Anatolia, designs in stone-carving, embroidery, miniature painting and most likely in rug-knotting.

In this collection of rugs, and in rugs known to the Data Bank of the Armenian Rugs Society, certain classic 19th century designs recur with such frequency it is clear they must be considered typically Armenian. The family of related *Vishapagorg* designs is one such group; the long Karabagh rugs with saw-toothed medallions outlined in bands of red is another. These are not "modern" or "debased" designs, but the worthy descendents of complex and ancient carpets, an integral part of Armenia's artistic tradition.

Another case in point is the Ottoman prayer rug, those exquisite "court rugs" woven in fine wool or silk in western Anatolia. That these beautiful rugs were woven by Ottoman craftsmen for the enjoyment of Ottoman patrons is unquestioned. But where did the designs come from? Central Asia? Look at Byzantine and Armenian miniature painting, from the 7th century on: page after page of arches supported by columns, with lamps hanging down, bushes growing up, supporting pairs of trees, all the stylistic vocabulary we have come to identify with Islamic Prayer rugs. Before it became the language of the Islamic Prayer rug, it was the language of the Eastern Christian miniature.

While writing this essay, I looked again at our Bursa silk prayer rug (Plate 1). The panel above the niche uses a design of grape vines, little birds looking up at grape bunches hanging down. I was reminded of the 6th century Armenian mosaic floor in Jerusalem which shows a vine springing up out of a vase (like the vase in the center of our prayer rug) and birds and grape bunches intertwined. The floor is a thousand years older than the rug, but the design is a survival, not a reinvention. It continued to be used in Armenian miniatures and carvings during the intervening centuries.

As more scholars from more diverse fields engage in the study of oriental rugs, our understanding of this pleasing and ancient art form will increase. It is clear that the study of oriental rugs goes beyond even the vast boundaries of the Islamic world. Questions will always remain. The study of history cannot claim to reveal an objective truth, but it can inspire us to think more deeply, and add to our appreciation of what we study. In this book it has not been our purpose to try and answer questions, only to suggest new ways they might be asked.

JOYCE GREGORIAN HAMPSHIRE
Newton Lower Falls
September 1986

# LIST OF PLATES

# SELECTED BIBLIOGRAPHY

ARMENIAN RUGS-THE GREGORIAN COLLECTION
  Lucy Der Manuelian                                ANN ARBOR 1983
CARPET MAGIC
  Jon Thompson                                      LONDON 1983
CAUCASIAN RUGS
  Ulrich Schurmann                                  BRAUNSCHWEIG n.d.
CAUCASIAN RUGS OF YESTERDAY
  Nicolas Fokker                                    LONDON 1979
THE EASTERN CARPET IN THE WESTERN WORLD
  Arts Council                                      LONDON 1983
THE GREGORIAN COLLECTION OF ARMENIAN RUGS
  Dartmouth College                                 NEWTON 1979
THE HISTORY OF THE EARLY TURKISH CARPET
  Kurt Erdmann                                      LONDON 1977
KAZAK
  Raoul Tschebull                                   NEW YORK 1971
ORIENTAL RUGS
  Murray L. Eiland                                  BOSTON 1976
ORIENTAL RUGS AND THE STORIES THEY TELL
  Arthur T. Gregorian                               NEW YORK 1978
RUGS & CARPETS FROM THE CAUCASUS
  Kerimov, Stepanian, Grigoliya, Tsitsishvili       LENINGRAD 1984
WEAVERS, MERCHANTS AND KINGS
  Der Manuelian, Eiland                             FORT WORTH 1984
ARMENIA: CRADLE OF CIVILIZATION
  David Marshall Lang                               LONDON 1970
ARMENIA: THE SURVIVAL OF A NATION
  Christopher J. Walker                             LONDON 1980
ARMENIA: TRAVELS AND STUDIES (2 Vols.)
  H.F.B. Lynch                                      BEIRUT 1967
ARMENIAN ART
  Sirarpie Der Nersessian                           PARIS 1977
THE ARMENIANS
  David Marshall Lang                               LONDON 1981